JOACHIM BERTHOLD

Mit allen guten Wünschen!
Sabine Berthold-Fordemann
20. Oktober 2017

Samuelis Baumgarte Galerie, Bielefeld
7. Oktober – 10. November 2007

JOACHIM BERTHOLD

KERBER

VORWORT

FOREWORD

Schon als Kind war ich jedes Mal beeindruckt, wenn mein Vater in seinem Atelier in Ton modellierte und später daraus eine Bronzeplastik entstand. Im sogenannten Atelierhaus in Oberaudorf im oberbayerischen Inntal aufgewachsen, erlebte ich die vielen Stimmungen, in denen mein Vater arbeitete, und seine überaus ernsthafte Auseinandersetzung mit seinem zentralen Thema „Der Mensch", im körperlichen wie im geistigen Sinn.

Je älter ich werde, desto mehr wachsen meine Begeisterung und das Verstehen seiner Werke. Antworten auf manche Fragen, die sich im Laufe meines Lebens ergeben haben, oder die ich ihm gerne noch stellen würde, finde ich immer wieder auch in der Betrachtung seiner Plastiken, beim Lesen seiner eigenen Schriften oder in Beiträgen anderer über ihn. Viele seiner Kunstfreunde, ob Schreibende oder ebenfalls Schaffende, habe ich in meinem Elternhaus kennengelernt, es herrschte oft ein sehr lebendiges und anregendes Miteinander.

Für meine Eltern waren die Zeiten wirtschaftlich nicht immer einfach. Es waren auch „Brotarbeiten" notwendig, aber mit bewundernswerter Geduld hielt mein Vater an seinem eigenen Schaffen fest, an seiner eigenen künstlerischen Entwicklung, kontinuierlich bis zu seinem Tod im Jahre 1990. Die neunzigste Wiederkehr seines Geburtstages, am 17. Oktober 1917, nehme ich dankbar zum Anlass für diese Ausstellung und den begleitenden, umfassenden Katalog zu seinem Werk.

Dass mein Mann Karl schon lange vor unserer gemeinsamen Zeit eine Skulptur meines Vaters für sich entdeckt hat, die ihn seit seiner Jugend fasziniert, war schon immer eine Besonderheit für uns. Für unsere beiden Söhne Johannes und Markus und für meine in den Vereinigten Staaten lebende Schwester mit ihren Söhnen Robert und Christopher ist es mir eine große Freude, die Werke ihres Großvaters wieder öffentlich zu zeigen.

Ihnen, der Leserin, dem Leser, wünsche ich, in Anlehnung an die Worte meines Vaters Joachim Berthold, dass die Betrachtung seiner Kunst zur Bereicherung Ihres Lebens beitragen möge.

Even as a child I was impressed every time my father made a clay model in his studio and then later a bronze sculpture was created out of it. Growing up in the so-called 'studio-house' in Oberaudorf in the Inn Valley in Upper Bavaria, I experienced the different moods in which my father worked and his invariably earnest engagement with his central theme – 'Man' – in both a physical and spiritual sense.

The older I get, the more my excitement for and understanding of his work grows. The answers to many questions which arose in the course of my life, or which I wish I could still ask him, are revealed to me when I study his sculptures, or read his own writings or what has been written about him. I got to know many of his artistic friends, whether writers or artists like himself, at my parents' home, which often made for an extremely lively and inspiring social setting.

For my parents, times were not always financially straightforward. It was also necessary to take on commissions just to get by, but with amazing determination my father stayed true to his own creative work, to his own artistic development, continuously up to his death in 1990. The ninetieth anniversary of his birth on October 17, 1917 is for me a welcome occasion for this exhibition and the accompanying comprehensive catalogue of his work.

That my husband Karl had already discovered a sculpture by my father, which had fascinated him since his youth, long before we came together, has always been a striking coincidence for us. For the sake of our two sons Johannes and Markus and for my sister in the United States with her sons Robert and Christopher, it is a great pleasure for me to show their grandfather's work in public again.

For you, the reader, I wish that, to borrow the words of my father Joachim Berthold, the contemplation of his art may help to enrich your life.

SABINE BERTHOLD-FORDEMANN

Verwandlung einer Kugel | *Transformation of a Sphere*, 1986/89, Bronze, h 77,5 cm

PLATOS PUPPE

Das Werk des Bildhauers
Joachim Berthold neu gesehen
Von Gerhard Charles Rump

PLATO'S PUPPET

The Work of the Sculptor
Joachim Berthold – A Reappraisal
By Gerhard Charles Rump

Eine der Bronzeplastiken von Joachim Berthold zeigt eine Scheibe (*Diskos*, 1979) mit dem Umfang eines 4/6-Kreises, aus der in der oberen Hälfte, wo das plastische Material fehlt, das die Scheibe vervollständigt hätte, eine Reihe von eleganten Figuren heraustritt, und wo jeder Körper den anderen gleichsam vor sich her schiebt, wie beim Nachwachsen der Zähne eines Hais.[1] Dieses Formprinzip, das zugleich ein Motiv darstellt, hat sich zu einem wiederkehrenden Thema in Bertholds Werk entwickelt. Andere Arbeiten ähnlicher Art, um nur zwei zu nennen, sind *Parabel* von 1981 und *Mauer V* aus dem Jahr 1983.[2] Sie stellen Varianten eines Themas vor. *Parabel* kann man als Darstellung eines Wechselspiels vollplastischen Volumens mit flachen Figuren sehen, die aus der Leere treten, aus einer negativen Form, die aber mehr Metall verbrauchen als es zur Füllung der Leere bedurft hätte. Sie fallen in angehaltener Bewegung fächerförmig aus ihrer Form. Man kann das auch in der umgekehrten Reihenfolge „lesen": Die Fächerfiguren falten sich zusammen, um aus der Leere hervorzukommen und in die vollplastische Form einzutreten. Wie auch immer: Der Betrachter wird hier auf eine nachdenkliche Reise durch den Prozess künstlerischen Schaffens geschickt, nicht nur den dieses speziellen Werkes, sondern überhaupt. In *Mauer V* zeigt sich die Reihe der Figuren als Folge hohler und gerundeter Formen, wo eine Hohlform in uneindeutigem Winkel schwebt, so dass man sagen kann, sie fällt oder steigt gleichzeitig.

Mauer V gehört zu einer Werkgruppe Bertholds, der *Menschenmauer*, in der er über den Schaffensprozess reflektiert und visualisiert, wie er es gesagt hat, ein bestimmtes Verhältnis von Gestalt und Form: „Die menschliche Gestalt ist in eine Form eingebunden, durchdringt sie, um sich dann völlig aus ihr herauszulösen."[3] Diese Serie hat mit der Berliner Mauer nichts zu tun. Sie

In one of Joachim Berthold's sculptures we see a bronze disc (*Diskos*, 1979), about four sixths of a circle in circumference, out of which, on the top half, where the material is 'missing' to make it a full disc, a line of elegantly abstracted figures emerges, every newly emerging body pushing its forerunner forward, like the replacement of sharks' teeth.[1] This formal principle, which is a motif at the same time, developed to become a recurrent subject in Berthold's work. Other works following this path, to name just two, are *Parable* (1981) and *Wall V* (1983).[2] They represent, of course, variations of the subject. *Parable* can be seen as staging an interplay of fully rounded volume and flat figures coming out of a void, a negative form, consuming more metal volume than the void, and falling from their mould in arrested motion, unfolding a fan of figures. One might 'read' it in the other direction as well: the fan figures fold together to step out of the void and join to form the fully rounded figure. Any which way one reads it, here the viewer is taken on a reflective journey through the conditions of the creative process, not only of this special work, but as such. In *Wall V* the row of people shows itself as a sequence of hollow and round forms, one hollow form hovering in

Diskos, 1979
Bronze, h 22 cm

7

stellt vielmehr ein Entwicklungsstadium in Bertholds Werk dar und ist, wenn man seine eigenen Worte dazu liest, eine rein ästhetische und formale Angelegenheit. Glücklicherweise ist das so, denn kaum jemand interessierte sich dafür, wäre es anders.

Das Thema begann mit der Skulptur einer Menschengruppe, der *Menschenmauer* von 1960 (Abb. S. 28/29) und einem Relief auf einem frei stehenden flachen Quader mit einem ähnlichen figürlichen Motiv (*Memento*) aus dem gleichen Jahr.[4] Die menschliche Mauer, mit Figuren, die dem Betrachter gegenüberstehen, zwingt ihn, eine Position für sich und auch die anderen zu bestimmen. Sie entwickelte sich zu einer frei stehenden Mauer mit den Figuren davor und auch dahinter, sowohl in hohlen als auch in vollplastischen Formen, die beide autonom dastehen, gezeigt im Prozess des Sich-Befreiens aus dem Material.

Zurück zum *Diskos*. Hier kann man an die russische Puppe denken, in der eine weitere Puppe steckt und in dieser noch eine andere („Matrioschka"). Aber da hat es noch mehr. Es ist nicht nur irgendeine Puppe, es ist sozusagen Platos Puppe, denn Berthold hat die menschliche Form beschrieben, wie sie sich aus dem umgebenden Material befreit. Und das geht ja nur, wenn sie, die Form, schon vorhanden ist. Und das ist genau das,

an ambiguous angle, so that one might say it is falling or it is rising at the same time.

Wall V belongs to a group of works, the *Human Wall* series, in which Berthold reflects on the creative process, visualising that 'the human figure is bound inside a form to completely step out of it.'[3] This series hasn't got anything to do with the Berlin Wall – it rather is a stage in the development of Joachim Berthold's oeuvre, and, if one reads him in his own words on the *Wall* series, a thoroughly aesthetic and formal affair. Luckily: hardly anybody would take interest in these works if they played just a political tune.

The whole subject started with a sculpture of a group of people, the *Human Wall* (Fig. pp. 28/29) of 1960, and a reliefon a free-standing slab with a similar motif (*Memento*) from the same year.[4] The human wall, the wall composed of people confronting the viewer, forcing him to define a position both for himself and the others, developed into a free-standing wall with people in front of it, and behind it, too, both in fully rounded and in hollow forms, both standing autonomously and caught in the act of freeing themselves from the material.

Coming back to the *Diskos,* one might think of the Russian puppets containing another puppet containing yet another puppet ('Matrioshki') – a very appropriate association. But there is more to it: it's not just a puppet, it's Plato's puppet, as Berthold described the human form freeing itself from the material it is bound to. It can only free itself from the surrounding material if it is already 'in there'. And this is exactly what Michelangelo (and a number of other sculptors) thought: form is inherent in the material, the artist 'only' has to free it from those fetters. Michelangelo is said to have answered the question, how difficult is it to carve a lion, by saying that it was very easy – all one had to do was to chip away everything that didn't resemble a lion.[5]

Mauer V | Wall V, 1982/83
Bronze, h 22 cm

was Michelangelo (und eine stattliche Reihe anderer Bildhauer) gedacht haben: Form ist dem Material inhärent, der Künstler braucht sie „nur" daraus zu befreien. Michelangelo wird nachgesagt, er hätte auf die Frage, wie schwer es sei, einen Löwen in einer Skulptur darzustellen, geantwortet, es sei ganz einfach – man müsse nur alles wegschlagen, was nicht nach Löwe aussähe.[5]

Die Idee, dass eine besondere Form schon im umgebenden Material vorhanden ist, und dass es dem Künstler obliegt, sie daraus zu befreien, ist eine neuplatonische Vorstellung. Der Neuplatonismus erlebte eine Wiedergeburt in der Renaissance, und man weiß, dass spätestens vom Quattrocento an solche Ideen auch in Künstlerkreisen lebhaft verhandelt wurden. Die neuplatonische Schule der Philosophie wird für gewöhnlich mit Ammonios Sakkas (172–242) von Alexandria und seinem Schüler Plotin in Verbindung gebracht. Dieser letzte große philosophische Systementwurf der Antike[6] sah die Welt als eine Emanation aus dem höchsten Prinzip an, was nach sich zog, auch niedriger angesiedelte oder niedrigere Prinzipien zuzulassen. Daraus folgte, dass jedes Prinzip auch ein Prinzip für etwas anderes ist. In diesem Lichte gesehen, stehen eine Reihe von Arbeiten Joachim Bertholds für neuplatonische philosophische Grundsätze und bilden daher so etwas wie Platos Puppe.

Natürlich lässt sich Joachim Bertholds Werk mit neuplatonischen Kategorien nicht vollständig erfassen, obwohl das Motiv der männlichen wie weiblichen hintereinander gestaffelten Figuren in seinem Œuvre immer wieder vorkommt. In diesem Zusammenhang wird die Frage wichtig, ob diese Figuren als „eine" oder als „viele" zu sehen sind. Ästhetisch betrachtet sind sie in der Tat viele Figuren, die je eine Phase der Entwicklung einer Figur repräsentieren, was wiederum bedeutet, dass sie eine einzige Figur sind, aufgefasst in verschiedenen Zuständen: Diese eine Figur, selbst als

This idea, that a specific form is already contained in the material and that it is the artist's task to bring it out, is a neoplatonic idea. Neoplatonism had a renaissance of its own in the Renaissance, and we know that from the Quattrocento onwards at the latest it was a subject discussed very vividly also in artistic circles. The neoplatonic school of philosophy is usually associated with Ammonios Sakkas (172–242) of Alexandria and his disciple Plotinos. This last great theory of ancient philosophy[6] saw the world as an emanation of a highest principle, which also meant that a 'higher' principle needed a 'lower' one, so that any given principle is always also a principle for something else. Seen this way, a number of works of Joachim Berthold exemplify neoplatonic philosophical principles. They constitute something like Plato's puppet.

The work of Joachim Berthold, of course, is not fully describable in neoplatonic terms, although the motif of the figures, both male and female, in echelon formation, can be found throughout Berthold's work. It is an important question in this context whether the figures are to be seen as one or as many. Aesthetically they are many, representing different stages of development of one, which means that they are one figure, seen in dif-

Skulptur, wird gesehen, wie sie sich durch den Raum und die Zeit bewegt. Denn wenn man sich nicht durch den Raum bewegt, bewegt man sich doch durch die Zeit. Und daran hat Berthold wohl gedacht, denn nach dem Zweiten Weltkrieg kam die Relativitätstheorie, die zwölf Jahre lang als hassenswert „jüdisch" gegolten hatte, wieder zu Ehren. Es gibt dennoch Unterschiede zwischen Bertholds Figur, dem *Nu descendant un escalier* von Marcel Duchamp, den Phasenbildern von Giacomo Balla und Eadweard Muybridges Chronophotographie.[7] Die letzteren drei sind eng miteinander verwandt, und es gibt Verbindungen zwischen Duchamp und Berthold. Man muss aber im Auge behalten, dass es sich bei Muybridge um dokumentarische Abbildungen handelt. Die einzelnen Aufnahmen, die einen Bewegungsprozess zergliedern, haben keinen Bildwert im künstlerischen Sinne. Balla unterscheidet sich von Duchamp dadurch, dass die Bewegungsphasen der Hundebeine keine unabhängigen Elemente darstellen. Sie können als einzelne Bildteile nicht den gleichen Rang im Bilde einnehmen, den sie zusammen beanspruchen. Bei Duchamp ist das anders: Jede Phase beim herabsteigenden Akt hat einen eigenen Bildwert, so wie das auch bei Berthold der Fall ist. Ein Unterschied besteht allerdings darin, dass man weder bei Berthold noch bei Duchamp eine autonome Figur ohne Unschärfen freilegen kann, aber prinzipiell stimmt es.

Ein weiteres bei Berthold stets wiederkehrendes Thema ist das der Gegensätze. Er stellt das Raue und das Polierte gegenüber, das Positive und das Negative, mit Relieffiguren, die zwischen diesen Polen vermitteln. Natürlich nicht unbedingt alles in einer Arbeit, aber auch das gibt es. Als Beispiel diene *Platz I.* Alle Elemente teilen sich die Grundplatte. Es gibt eine Mauer mit Relieffiguren, zumeist in Hohlform. Es gibt einen Quader und eine vollplastische Figur und auf der anderen Seite der Mauer eine Kugel. Die Zweiteilung des Mauer-Elements

ferent stages: the one figure is, even as a sculpted one, seen moving through space and time. If you are not moving through space, you still are moving through time: this probably also was in Berthold's mind as after WW II, relativity had come back into people's minds in Germany after having been ridiculed as obnoxiously Jewish for twelve years. Still, there are differences between Berthold's figure, the *Nu descendant un escalier* by Duchamp, the phase images of Balla and Eadweard Muybridge's chronophotography.[7] The latter three are very closely related, and there are links between Duchamp and Berthold. But one must keep in mind that Muybridge is depiction: the single shots analysing a process of motion do not possess pictorial value in an artistic sense. Balla differs from Duchamp in that the phases of a dog's leg are not independent items – they cannot as single elements take the same position in the painting as they do together. In Duchamp this is different: each single phase in the *Descending Nude* is of independent pictorial value. And this is also the case in Berthold's work. The twist: neither in Berthold nor in Duchamp can one really single out a phase without blurring the edges, but 'in principle' it works.

Another recurrent theme in Berthold's oeuvre is oppositions. He opposes the rough and the polished and the hollow and the fully rounded figure, with relief fig-

Platz I | Place I, 1969,
Bronze, h 89 cm

Schreitender III
Pacing Man III, 1979
Bronze, h 43,5 cm

in Mauer und Quader sorgt für ästhetische Spannung. Dies findet sowohl formal wie ästhetisch ein Echo, wenn auch in einer Variante, in der Dichotomie der positiven wie negativen Volumina und der rauen wie polierten (Kugel-)Oberflächen. Wir finden hierin einen Ausdruck der unterschiedlichen Charaktere der plastischen Elemente. Obwohl es Berthold hier um einen Platz, einen städtischen Raum geht, was auch bei Giacometti vorkommt, ist er doch weit weg von allem, was Giacometti bewegt hat. Giacometti erscheint wie ein gleichzeitig sowohl konzeptueller als auch visueller Bildhauer, der sich wenig um Volumina kümmerte, aber einheitliche Oberflächen anstrebte. Berthold hingegen konzentriert sich auf die plastischen Werte, auf Dreidimensionalität und unterschiedliche Oberflächen. Die Differenzierung der Oberflächen kommt zumeist sogar innert einer einzigen Figur vor, wie etwa beim *Schreitenden III* von 1979.[8]

Wir sehen also, dass es Berthold um das Wesen der Dinge geht. Er ist weniger auf die Erscheinung aus. Seine Figuren sind verallgemeinerte Darstellungen, nicht definierte Individuen. Das ist wichtig zu berücksichtigen, um zu verstehen, auf welcher Ebene Berthold die Diskussion führt. Es geht ihm nicht um dieses hier und jenes dort, um das Leben, die Liebe, das Hassen und den Tod von Menschen. Leben und Schicksal, Geschichte und Entwicklung werden nicht anhand individueller Beispiele thematisiert, in deren erzählten Geschichten.

ures mediating between the extremes. Not necessarily, though, within the frame of one distinct work, but there are works of that kind. A case in point is *Place I.* All elements share a common plinth. There is a wall with figures in relief, mostly hollow. There is an ashlar (cuboid; 'column' with square section) and a fully formed figure; on the other side of the wall element we see a ball. The division of the wall element in two – the wall and the ashlar – provides an aesthetic tension. This is echoed both formally and, aesthetically, albeit in a variation, by the dichotomies of positive and negative volume and rough and polished (ball) surface. This relates to the different characters of the sculptural elements. Although Berthold presents a place, an urban space, like Giacometti did, he is far away from anything Giacometti was moved by. Giacometti seems to be both a conceptual and a 'visual' sculptor, paying little attention to volume and striving to find a unified surface. Berthold concentrates on the plastic values, on volume and differentiated surfaces. The differentiation of surfaces is, more often than not, to be found on one single figure, like, for instance, on *Pacing Man III,* 1979.[8]

We can see, therefore, that Joachim Berthold attempts to find the heart of things. He is less concerned about appearance. His figures are generalised images of man, not particular individuals. This is important, as it shows the level on which Berthold discusses things. He doesn't tell a tale of many cities, in which people live, love, hate and die. Life and fate, history and development are not exemplified by individual lives the story of which is told. Instead Berthold unfolds the principles his puppets have to follow.[9]

Stattdessen entfaltet Berthold das Panorama der Prinzipien, denen seine Puppen unterworfen sind.[9]

Sein formales Vokabular ist ineinander verwoben und von logischen Zusammenhängen geprägt. Das gibt ihm die praktisch unbegrenzte Freiheit, sich im Medium der Skulptur auszudrücken. Es gibt nichts, was er nicht kann, und von daher braucht nichts ungesagt zu bleiben. Bertholds breite Palette an Kompositionsformen funktioniert dabei als Plattform universaler Kommunikation. Alle denkbaren Variationen sind auch möglich, vorausgesetzt, sie folgen den Regeln skulpturaler Gestaltung.[10] Wie Gerhard Kolberg gesagt hat: „Seine plastischen Schöpfungen sind als Summe zahlreicher Schaffensideen und intuitiver Impulse zu betrachten."[11]

Eine wichtige Werkgruppe sind Bertholds Stelen. Ein sehr klassisches Thema und kein einfaches. Die inhärente Linearität der Stele wird stets den skulpturalen Bemühungen Widerstand entgegensetzen, und die Faszination einer wohlgestalteten Stele liegt gerade in der Balance zwischen der dynamisch aufstrebenden Vertikalität und den skulpturalen Interventionen. Eine Stele stellt dem Betrachter auch ein abstraktes Gegenüber zur Verfügung, einen Partner in einem ästhetischen Dialog, dessen Charakter als definiertes Kunstwerk Form und Erscheinung zur gleichen Zeit darstellt. Stelen sind

His formal vocabulary is interrelated and logically connected. This gives him practically unlimited freedom to express himself in the medium of sculpture: there is nothing he can't do, so there is nothing unsaid he wants to say. Also his wide variety of compositional patterns provides a platform of universal communication. All thinkable variations are possible, provided they follow the rules of a sculptural framework.[10] As Gerhard Kolberg has said, 'His sculptural creations must be seen as the sum of numerous logical creative ideas and intuitive impulses.'[11]

An important group are Berthold's stelai. This is a highly classical sculptural theme, and not an easy one. The inherent linearity of a stele will always counteract any sculptural endeavour, and the fascination of a well formed stele lies exactly in the balance between the dynamic and soaring verticality and the sculptural interventions. A stele is also a very abstract counterpart of the viewer – a partner in aesthetic dialogue whose character as a defined work of art is form and appearance at the same time. Stelai are the totem poles of Western Art, in fact they – especially those of Joachim Berthold – are aesthetically and conceptually nearer the tribal models than their precursors in ancient art. Ancient stelai bear more resemblance to tombstones.

Each of Berthold's stelai is a variation on the subject, and some of them aren't true stelai. They are 'something-like-a-stele'. The *Torso IV* (1976) is a lot in that number.[12] The larger-than-life female figure, half hollow-form, half positive volume, is emerging from a block her own size. There is too much aesthetic autonomy in the block for the work to count as a stele, yet there are enough characteristics to include it. Maybe this makes it all the more interesting. The *Runner* of the same year, however, will have to be counted out, as the striding leg makes for too much space-gain for the work to be a stele.[13] *Female Statue III*, contrariwise, despite the chain dangling from the hips, is a true, formally constrained and contained

Paar VII, | *Couple VII,* 1979
Bronze, h 100 cm

die Totempfähle der Kunst des Westens, in der Tat sind sie – vor allem die von Joachim Berthold – diesen ästhetisch wie konzeptuell näher als ihren Vorgängern in der Antike, die uns zu oft an Grabsteine erinnern.

Jede von Bertholds Stelen stellt eine eigene Variation des Themas dar. Manche sind keine „echten" Stelen, sondern „stelenartige" Skulpturen. Dazu gehört etwa *Torso IV* von 1976.[12] Die überlebensgroße weibliche Figur, halb Hohlform, halb Vollplastik, tritt aus einem Block ihrer Größe heraus. Die ästhetische Autonomie des Blockes ist zu groß, um als Stele gelten zu können, und dennoch gibt es stelenhafte Eigenschaften. Vielleicht macht gerade das dieses Werk so aufmerksamkeitsstark. Der *Läufer* aus dem gleichen Jahr gehört nicht dazu, denn der Ausfallschritt bewirkt zuviel Raumgewinn, um hier noch von einer Stele sprechen zu können.[13] *Weibliche Statue III* hingegen, trotz der an der Hüfte hängenden Kette, ist eine echte, formal reduzierte und kompakte Stele, die den Betrachter mit einem archaischen, augenlosen Blick gegenübertritt. Eine Göttin, ein fernes Idealbild, ein Wirklichkeit werdender Traum. Die Kette ruft eine Zahl wild disparater Gedankenverbindungen hervor, denn sie wird von einer präzisen Besonderheit bestimmt. Aber die Figur ist mehr, stärker verallgemeinert und flüchtiger. Der Gegensatz zwischen der Kette als Spezifischem und der Figur als Allgemeinem ruft die bezirzende Spannung in diesem Werk hervor.

Eine besonders atemberaubende Variation ist das *Paar VII* aus dem Jahr 1979, monumental in der Wirkung, obwohl nur 100 cm hoch. Wir sehen wirklich ein Paar, jede Figur eine Stele für sich, zusammen aber formen sie ein allgemeingültiges Bild einer menschlichen Figur, jede als Bein einer abstrahierten menschlichen Figur im Sinne eines Superzeichens. Andere Stelen, wie zum Beispiel *Männliche Statue I* (Abb. S. 75) aus dem Jahr 1981 und *Weibliche Statue IV* (Abb. S. 74) aus dem gleichen Jahr[14] formulieren Figurationen innerhalb der Begrenzungen

stele confronting the viewer with an archaic, eyeless look. A goddess, an ideal aloof, a dream becoming form. The chain evokes a number of wildly disparate associations, as it is dominated by a precise distinctiveness. The chain is a chain is a chain. But the figure is more, more generalized, and more elusive. So the opposition between the chain (specific) and the figure (general) accounts for a lot of the intriguing tension in the work.

A very special and breathtaking variation is *Couple VII* of 1979, monumental despite its height of only three feet plus. We do see a couple, each figure a stele of its own, but together they form a general image of man, being the legs of a super-sign type of an abstracted human figure. Other stelai, like *Male statue I* (Fig. p. 75) of 1981 and *Female Statue IV* (Fig. p. 74) of the same year[14] formulate figuration within the aesthetic barrier of the cylinder. This is also the case in *Cylinder* of 1981, which combines the stele with the emerging figures[15] and, in an especially happy solution, in *Male-female stele,* also from the year 1981. In this work, the two figures share the same cylinder, each facing away from each other. A stele combining Berthold's subjects of the human figure and the material block out of which it emerges is *Trias* (1989, just 22 cms / 9.5 ins high). This all shows, how

eines Zylinders. Das ist auch bei der *Zylinder* (1981) genannten Arbeit der Fall, die die Stele mit der hervortretenden Figur kombiniert.[15] Als besonders glückliche Lösung mag *Männlich-Weibliche Stele* (1981) gelten. In dieser Arbeit teilen sich die beiden Figuren den Zylinder, blicken aber in entgegengesetzte Richtungen. Eine Stele, in der Berthold seine Themen der menschlichen Figur und des Blocks, aus dem sie heraustritt, vereint finden wir in *Trias* (1989, nur 22 cm hoch). All das zeigt, wie „verdammt variabel"[16] Joachim Berthold als Bildhauer ist. Aber man kann hier auch Vorverweise auf oder Verbindungen zur zeitgenössischen Kunst finden.

Natürlich ist das Œuvre von Joachim Berthold ein abgeschlossenes Kapitel insofern als keine neuen Arbeiten jemals hinzukommen werden. Was aber den dauernden Wert seines ästhetischen Beitrags betrifft, die Anwendbarkeit seiner ästhetischen Prinzipien innerhalb eines zeitgenössischen Diskurses, so gibt es wohl mehr Verbindungen, die ins 21. Jahrhundert zeigen, als solche, die auf Vergangenes verweisen. Das kann man am Thema der Stele im Werk zeitgenössischer Künstler gut nachvollziehen, aber auch andere Prinzipien seiner Kunst leben in der zeitgenössischen Kunst weiter.

Ganz offensichtlich gibt es die meisten Ähnlichkeiten mit Joachim Berthold bei Eva Drewett. Geboren 1957 in Polen, kam sie 1979 nach England und studierte dort unter anderem am Royal College of Art. Über sie schrieb Ann Elliot: „Meistens in Bronze arbeitend … nutzt Eva Drewett die menschliche Gestalt um eine kraftvolle Botschaft zu vermitteln."[17] Man sieht eine Ähnlichkeit in der Anschauung ebenso wie in der technischen Arbeitsweise. Das bedeutet nicht, dass Drewett aus Bertholds Werk zitiert, aber die wichtige Tatsache wird deutlich, dass Bertholds Vision der Bildhauerei auch im Zeitgenössischen Mitstreiter hat. Ein anderer Bruder im Geiste ist der 1965 geborene Hans Schüle, der in München und Berlin studiert hat. In einigen seiner

'damn various'[16] Joachim Berthold is as a sculptor. But it can also serve as a link to contemporary art.

Joachim Berthold's work is, of course, a closed chapter in so far as no more new works will ever be added to the oeuvre. But as far as the continuing value of his aesthetic contribution is concerned – the applicability of his artistic principles within the context of a contemporary discourse – there are more links to the art of the 21st Century than to past eras. This is most easily exemplified by looking at the treatment of the stele subject by contemporary artists, but, also, principles governing his other works are alive and well in contemporary art.

The sculptor whose works resemble Berthold's sculptures most is, pretty obviously, Eva Drewett. She was born in Poland in 1957, came to England in 1979 and studied at, among other places, the Royal College of Art. 'Working mostly in bronze … Eva Drewett uses the human form to convey a powerful message' says Ann Elliot.[17] One finds a set of similar views and techniques. This doesn't mean that Drewett quotes from Berthold, rather we see the important message that Berthold's

Zylinder | Cylinder, 1980/81
Bronze, h 73,5 cm

Werke, wie *Curve* (2005; geschmiedeter Stahl), folgen sowohl die Gesamtform wie die Variationen von positiver und negativer Form den gleichen Entscheidungen, die auch Berthold getroffen hat. Marc Wellmann beschrieb das Werk von Hans Schüle wie folgt: „Plastische Gestalt, Material und handwerkliche Bearbeitung: in dieser Reihenfolge lassen sich Schüles Skulpturen lesen."[18] Diese Beschreibung bliebe zutreffend, wendete sie man auf Berthold an. Das heißt aber keinesfalls, dass wir hier mit Binsenweisheiten handeln, sondern vielmehr, dass es hier um ästhetische Prinzipien geht, die die Zeiten unverletzt passieren, die wiederkehren, und die so eine chronologische Rekurrenz ähnlicher oder sogar identischer Phänomene etablieren.

Auch Isa Genzken, die 2007 Deutschland auf der Biennale in Venedig vertrat, hat eine Reihe von Werken geschaffen, in denen sie bestimmte plastische Methoden aufgriff, besonders das negative Volumen, um skulpturale Form zu definieren und zu akzentuieren. Ihr *Ellipsoid Zwilling* von 1982 besteht aus zwei schlanken ellipsoiden Formen, farbig gefasst, je sechs Meter lang, deren Oberfläche teilweise durch negative Volumina virtualisiert wird.[19] Es ist wichtig zu sehen, dass zeitgenössische Künstler solche Methoden anwenden. Das beweist nämlich, dass es in Ästhetik und Form Kontinuitäten gibt, und dass jegliche zukünftige Kunst noch der *conditio humana* verbunden sein wird. Entweder wird sie eine neue Geschichte auf alte Weise erzählen oder eine alte Geschichte mit neuen Worten. Und wenn es eine neue Geschichte sein sollte, auf neue Weise vorgebracht, so wird sie doch einer bekannten Grammatik folgen.

Es mag eigenartig oder weit hergeholt erscheinen, aber es gibt auch Ähnlichkeiten mit dem Werk von Albert Hien.[20] Um das erkennen zu können, muss man den Blick von den Oberflächen und Motiven weglenken, hin auf die Tiefenstruktur von Hiens Werk. Da wird man dann wieder auf die Beziehungen zwischen positiven

sculptural vision has its partners also in contemporary art. Another brother spirit is Hans Schüle, born 1965, who studied in Munich and Berlin. In some of his works, like *Curve* (2005, forged steel) both the overall shape and the variations of positive and negative forms follow decisions taken in the way Berthold took his. Marc Wellmann explained the work of Hans Schüle saying 'plastic shape, material and craftsmanship in treatment: in this order one can read Schüle's sculptures.'[18] This statement would remain true if one exchanged Schüle for Berthold. This does not mean that we are dealing with truisms, but that there are references to aesthetic principles, which pass the branes of time unharmed, which reoccur, establishing a chronological recurrence of similar or even identical phenomena.

Also Isa Genzken, who represented Germany at the 2007 Venice Biennale, created a number of works in which she used certain sculptural methods, in this case the negative volume, to define and accentuate sculptural form. Her *Ellipsoid Zwilling* (Ellipsoid twin) from the year 1982 consists of two slender ellipsoid shapes, coloured, about 22 feet long, the surface of which is partly virtualised by negative volume.[19] It is important to notice that contemporary artists use such methods. It proves that there is a continuity in aesthetics and form, and that any future art will still be linked to the human condition. Either it will tell a new story using old words or tell an old story in new words. And if it tells a new story in new words, it will still resort to a known grammar.

Strange and far-fetched as it may seem, there are also similarities with the work of Albert Hien.[20] To appreciate this, one will have turn one's eyes away from the motifs and surfaces and look at the deep structure of Hien's works. Then one will discover the intricate relationships between positive and negative volumes, fully formed and hollow forms, insides and outsides which govern Hien's works very much in the same way these categories ruled what came forth in Berthold's sculp-

und negativen Volumina, Hohl- und vollplastischen Formen, Innen- und Außenflächen stoßen, die für Hiens Arbeiten ebenso bestimmend sind wie diese Kategorien das bestimmten, was aus Bertholds kreativem Geist entstand. Es gibt in der Kunstgeschichte durchaus Beispiele für solche strukturellen Kontinuitäten. Als Kurt Schwitters seine Collagen schuf, benutzte er Alltagsmaterialien wie Bahnbillets und dergleichen, aber er hielt sich streng an die klassischen Kompositionsregeln, die schon für die Kunst der Alten Meister verbindlich waren. Später hat dann Robert Rauschenberg unter dem Einfluss von Schwitters gestanden, jedenfalls was das Benutzen von alltäglichen Materialien und Gegenständen anging, aber er folgte Schwitters nicht in Fragen der Komposition. Auf ähnliche Weise mag man sich das Gleiten durch verschiedene Ebenen ästhetischer Entwicklungen von Berthold bis Hien vorstellen. Es gibt auch eine Reihe ästhetischer Beziehungen zum Werk von Peter Burke, besonders was die Nutzung negativer Volumina zur Figurenkonstitution betrifft.[21]

Wie aktuell Joachim Berthold ist, zeigen seine Stelen. Sie sind keinesfalls Zeugen eines vergangenen Geschmacks, vielmehr weisen sie ein allgemeines Bedürfnis nach Vertikalität nach, ein Verlangen nach einem quasi-menschlichen Partner im ästhetischen Dialog. Es gibt heute sehr viele Bildhauer, die Stelen produzieren, von Stephan Huber[22] und Cosima von Bonin[23] bis Trupti Patel[24] – alle drei mit figurativem Element –, und von Raffael Rheinsberg[25] zu William Pye,[26] wobei die Letztgenannten eher abstrakt, „pur", arbeiten.

tures. There are examples of this structural continuity in art before. When Kurt Schwitters made his collages, he used everyday materials like train tickets and the like, but he strictly followed the classical rules of composition, which had already been relevant for the Art of the Old Masters. Robert Rauschenberg, subsequently, was influenced by Schwitters in so far that he used everyday materials and objects for his work, but he did not follow Schwitters in questions of composition. In a similar way one can imagine the slide through the levels of aesthetic development from Berthold to Hien. There are also a number of aesthetic relationships to the work of Peter Burke, especially in the use of the negative volume to create figures.[21]

A striking example for Joachim Berthold's being up to date are his stelai. They are in no way examples of a bygone taste, rather they exemplify a general desire for at least a certain amount of verticality, a desire to confront a sculpture as one's quasi-human partner in the aesthetic dialogue. There are very many artists producing stelai today, from Stephan Huber[22] and Cosima von Bonin[23] to Trupti Patel[24] – all three with some kind of 'figurative' touch – and from Raffael Rheinsberg[25] to William Pye,[26] the latter two in a more abstract, 'pure' form.

In Joachim Berthold's works we encounter a highly elegant, polished, thorough kind of sculpture, which has, of course, its roots in the past, but which formulates general concepts of creation, creativity, man and mankind which change little as they pass through the ages. What makes Berthold's works so fascinating is that he also points to the future, and that many of his sculptural principles can be seen in contemporary art, and not in a general, a common sense, not as a truism in any way, rather in an indispensable manner to bring out what is contained within the artist's materials – and in his mind.

In Joachim Bertholds Œuvre begegnet uns eine sehr elegante, glanzvolle und durchgearbeitete Bildhauerei, die selbstverständlich in der Vergangenheit wurzelt, die aber allgemeine Konzepte des Schöpferischen formuliert, von Kreativität, vom Menschen und der Menschheit, die sich über die Zeiten hinweg wenig verändern. Das Faszinierende an Bertholds Werk aber ist, dass es auch zukunftweisend ist und dass viele der skulpturalen Prinzipien, die er angewendet hat, auch in der zeitgenössischen Kunst eine Rolle spielen – und das nicht in einem allgemeinen, gewöhnlichen Sinne, nicht als bewährte „Binsen", sondern vielmehr als unverzichtbare Art, das herauszubringen, was in des Künstlers Material steckt – und in seinem Geist.

Aus dem Englischen übersetzt vom Autor

1   *Joachim Berthold.* Mit Beiträgen von Wilhelm F. Arntz und anderen, München: Hirmer 1987, Nr. 61, S. 145 (hiernach BERTHOLD 1987; dieses Buch begleitete die Retrospektive in der Städtischen Galerie Rosenheim, vom 21. August bis 4. Oktober 1987, aus Anlass von Bertholds 70. Geburtstag)

2   *Parabel:* BERTHOLD 1987, Nr. 71, S. 163; *Mauer V:* Berthold 1987, Nr. 76, S. 173

3   JOACHIM BERTHOLD, „Die Idee der Menschenmauern. Die *Mauer* von 1968", in: BERTHOLD 1987, S. 17–24, hier S. 19

4   BERTHOLD 1987, S. 18

5   Sir Edwin Henry Landseer soll das auch in Bezug auf seine Löwen am Trafalgar Square gesagt haben

6   WERNER BEIERWALTES, *Denken des Einen. Studien zur neuplatonischen Philosophie und ihrer Wirkungsgeschichte,* Frankfurt am Main: Klostermann 1985; HANS JOACHIM STÖRIG, *Kleine Weltgeschichte der Philosophie,* Frankfurt am Main: Fischer 1969, Bd. 1, S. 204–207, 287–288; ERNST HOFFMANN, *Platon. Eine Einführung in sein Philosophieren,* Reinbek: Rowohlt 1961, S. 16, 27, 67; JOHN GREGORY, *The neoplatonists. A reader,* London: Routledge 1999

7   PATRICK WALDBERG, *Der Surrealismus,* Köln: DuMont 1965; MAURICE NADEAU, *Geschichte des Surrealismus,* Reinbek: Rowohlt 1965; CHRISTA BAUMGARTH, *Geschichte des Futurismus,* Reinbek: Rowohlt 1966; WINFRIED NERDINGER, „Die Montage der Wirklichkeit", in: WERNER BUSCH (Hg.), *Funkkolleg Kunst. Eine Geschichte der Kunst im Wandel ihrer Funktionen,* München/Zürich: Piper 1987, Bd. 2, S. 765–792; GERHARD CHARLES RUMP, „Francis Bacons Menschenbild", in: *Kunstpsychologie, Kunst und Psychoanalyse, Kunstwissenschaft. Psychologische, anthropologische, semiotische Versuche zur Kunstwissenschaft,* Hildesheim/New York: Olms 1981, S. 146–168

8   *Joachim Berthold. 5. Juli–5. August 1990,* Ausst.-Kat. Haus am Lützowplatz, Berlin, 1990 (hiernach Berthold 1990), S. 41

9   Vgl. hierzu auch Gerhard Kolbergs Essay über Berthold, dessen Titel Bertholds Skulpturen als „Metaphern der menschlichen Existenz" benennt: GERHARD KOLBERG, „Joachim Bertholds Skulpturen als Metaphern der menschlichen Existenz", in: BERTHOLD 1990, S. 7–13

10   Vgl. hierzu ULRICH GERTZ, „Gedanken zur Kunst Joachim Bertholds", in: BERTHOLD 1987, S. 7–9

11   GERHARD KOLBERG (wie Anm. 9), S. 7

12   BERTHOLD 1990, S. 35

13   BERTHOLD 1990, S. 37

14   BERTHOLD 1990, S. 48

15   BERTHOLD 1990, S. 50

16   Gainsboroughs Ausruf, als er eine Ausstellung seines Rivalen Reynolds besuchte

17   ANN ELLIOT, „Biographies and texts", in: *Sculpture at Goodwood. A vision for twenty-first century British sculpture. Sculpture at Goodwood,* 2002, S. 347–348; S. 10–13

18   MARC WELLMANN, „Hans Schüle", in: *Die Macht des Dinglichen. Skulptur heute!,* Köln: Wienand 2007, S. 108–111, hier S. 111

19   KARIN THOMAS, *Kunst in Deutschland seit 1945,* Köln: Dumont 2002, S. 404

20   THOMAS (wie Anm. 19), S. 408

21   *Sculpture at Goodwood* (wie Anm. 17), S. 226–229, 333–334

22   THOMAS (wie Anm. 19), S. 408

23   THOMAS (wie Anm. 19), S. 483

24   *Sculpture at Goodwood* (wie Anm. 17), S. 162, 386

25   THOMAS (wie Anm. 19), S. 394

26   *Sculpture at Goodwood* (wie Anm. 17), S. 288, 387–389

1   *Joachim Berthold.* With essays by Wilhelm F. Arntz et al., Hirmer, Munich 1987, No 61, p. 145 (hereafter BERTHOLD 1987; this book accompanied the retrospective in the Städtische Galerie Rosenheim from August 21st to October 4th, 1987, to celebrate Berthold's 70th birthday)

2   *Parabel:* BERTHOLD 1987, No 71, p. 163; *Mauer V:* BERTHOLD 1987, No 76, p. 173

3   JOACHIM BERTHOLD, "Die Idee der Menschenmauern. Die *Mauer* von 1968", in: BERTHOLD 1987, pp. 17–24, here p. 19; quote translated

4   BERTHOLD 1987, p. 18

5   Sir Edwin Landseer is said to have used this quote referring to his Trafalgar Square lions

6   See WERNER BEIERWALTES, *Denken des Einen. Studien zur neuplatonischen Philosophie und ihrer Wirkungsgeschichte,* Klostermann, Frankfurt am Main, 1985; HANS JOACHIM STÖRIG, *Kleine Weltgeschichte der Philosophie,* Fischer, Frankfurt am Main, Hamburg, 1969, vol. 1, pp. 204–207; see also pp. 287–288; ERNST HOFFMANN, *Platon. Eine Einführung in sein Philosophieren,* Rowohlt, Reinbek 1961, pp. 16, 27, 67; JOHN GREGORY, *The Neoplatonists. A reader,* Routledge, London 1999

7   See PATRICK WALDBERG, *Der Surrealismus,* Du Mont, Cologne 1965; MAURICE NADEAU, *Geschichte des Surrealismus,* Rowohlt, Reinbek 1965; CHRISTA BAUMGARTH, *Geschichte des Futurismus,* Rowohlt, Reinbek 1966; WINFRIED NERDINGER, "Die Montage der Wirklichkeit", in: WERNER BUSCH (ed.), *Funkkolleg Kunst. Eine Geschichte der Kunst im Wandel ihrer Funktionen,* Piper, Munich and Zurich 1987, vol. 2, pp. 765–792; GERHARD CHARLES RUMP, "Francis Bacons Menschenbild", in: *Kunstpsychologie, Kunst und Psychoanalyse, Kunstwissenschaft. Psychologische, anthropologische, semiotische Versuche zur Kunstwissenschaft,* Olms, Hildesheim and New York 1981, pp. 146–168

8   See *Joachim Berthold,* 5. Juli – 5. August 1990, Haus am Lützowplatz, Berlin 1990 (hereafter BERTHOLD 1990), p. 41

9   This goes together well with Gerhard Kolberg's essay on Berthold, the title of which names Berthold's sculptures as 'metaphors of human existence'; GERHARD KOLBERG, "Joachim Bertholds Skulpturen als Metaphern der menschlichen Existenz", in: BERTHOLD 1990, pp. 7–13

10   See the appreciation of Berthold's works by ULRICH GERTZ, "Gedanken zur Kunst Joachim Bertholds", in: BERTHOLD 1987, pp. 7–9

11   GERHARD KOLBERG, op. cit., p. 7 (translated)

12   BERTHOLD 1990, p. 35

13   BERTHOLD 1990, p. 37

14   BERTHOLD 1990, p. 48

15   BERTHOLD 1990, p. 50

16   Gainsborough's famous exclamation on visiting an exhibition of his rival, Reynolds

17   ANN ELLIOT, "Biographies and texts", in: *Sculpture at Goodwood. A vision for twenty-first century British sculpture. Sculpture at Goodwood,* 2002, pp. 347–348; pp. 10–13

18   MARC WELLMANN, "Hans Schüle", in: *Die Macht des Dinglichen. Skulptur heute!,* Wienand, Cologne 2007, pp. 108–111, here p. 111 (translated)

19   KARIN THOMAS, *Kunst in Deutschland seit 1945,* Dumont, Cologne 2002, p. 404

20   THOMAS, op. cit., p. 408

21   *Sculpture at Goodwood,* pp. 226–229, 333–334

22   THOMAS, op. cit., p. 408

23   THOMAS, op. cit., p. 483

24   *Sculpture at Goodwood,* pp. 162, 386

25   THOMAS, op. cit., p. 394

26   *Sculpture at Goodwood,* pp. 288, 387–389

ABBILDUNGEN | ILLUSTRATIONS

ABBILDUNGEN | ILLUSTRATIONS

Jüngling | Youngling, 1958, Bonze, h 28 cm

Biest | Beast, 1959, Bronze, h 17 cm

Flügelwesen | Winged Creatures, 1959, Bronze, h 40 cm

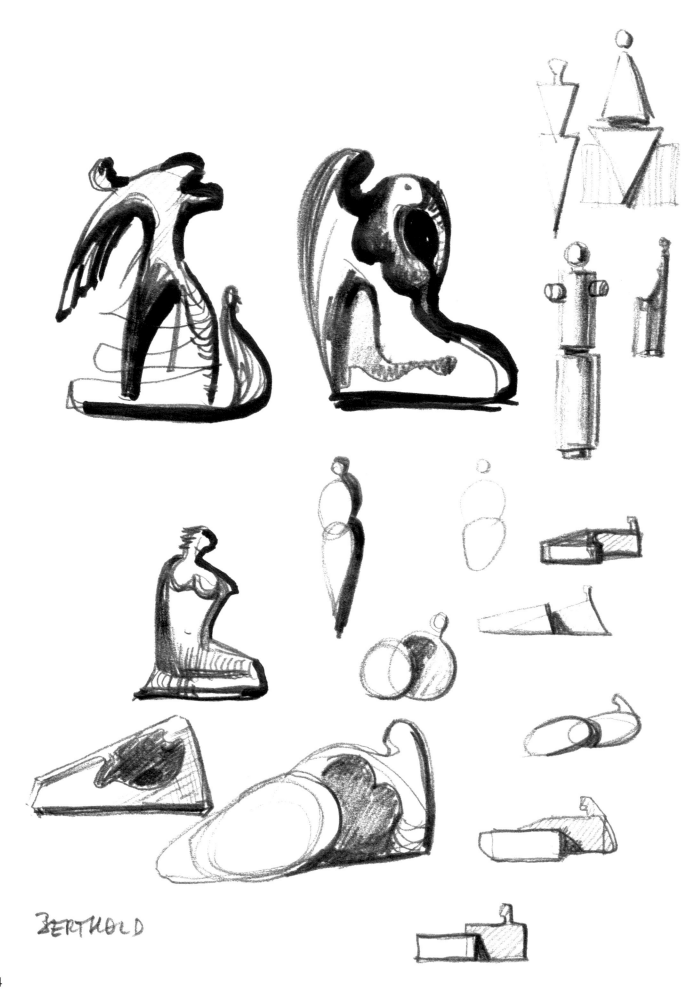

BERTHOLD

„Der Möglichkeiten, der menschlichen Figur Gestalt zu geben, sind ungeheuer viele. Allein die Vorstellung, daß Jahrtausende hindurch aus ihr ständig neue und andersartige Formen entwickelt wurden, ist erregend; Formen, die den Menschen darstellen und die durch ihre Eigenheiten bestimmte Ausdrucksgehalte oder Inhalte vermitteln. Es wäre sehr kühn zu behaupten, daß diese Möglichkeiten erschöpft seien, so kühn wie die Behauptung, daß der Mensch völlig erforscht, völlig klar vor uns stehe, alles ihn Bestimmende und Ausmachende bekannt und daher der Darstellung nicht mehr würdig sei. Der Mensch ist noch immer das Unbekannteste unserer Welt – ich bin der Ansicht, daß sein Erscheinungsbild dem Geist entspricht, der sein Wesen bildet, so wie alle Erscheinungen in der Natur ihrem Wesen entsprechen. Dazu kommt, daß die menschliche Gestalt eminent plastisch ist. Sie gibt durch Rumpf und Gliedmaßen die Möglichkeit, vielfältige plastische Gebilde zu schaffen, sei es eine Stele – eine stehende Figur – statisch und ruhig, sei es eine Raumplastik, die mit ihren Armen und Beinen einen Raum umschlingt, sei es eine Plastik, die das Moment der Bewegung besitzt. Dabei ist stets die spannungsvolle Möglichkeit gegeben, Seinszustände des Menschen – das Ewig-Menschliche – auszudrücken, deren Vielfalt auch nicht zu erschöpfen ist."

'There are a huge number of ways to give form to the human figure. Even just the thought that for thousands of years new and different forms have constantly arisen from it is an inspiration – forms which represent the person and which communicate particular expressions or contents through the special characteristics of the human figure. It would be very clever to insist that these possibilities have been exhausted, as clever as the claim that the human being has been completely studied, and appears before us completely clearly, that everything that determines and identifies the human is known and that therefore people are no longer worthy subjects of representation. The human being remains the most unknown thing in our world – I take the view that Man's appearance corresponds to the spirit that forms his essence, just as all phenomena in nature correspond to their essence. In addition, the human form is above all plastic. Through the torso and limbs it offers the possibility of creating complex plastic constructs, whether a stele – a standing figure – static and at rest, or a sculptured space which embraces a space with its arms and legs, or a sculpture that captures the moment of movement. In all this there is always the highly charged possibility of expressing the state of being of a human – the eternally human – the complexity of which will never be exhausted.'

JOACHIM BERTHOLD, 30. März | March 30, 1959

Schatten | Shadows, 1961, Bronze, h 44 cm

Karyatide I | *Caryatide I*, 1960, Bronze, h 28,5 cm

Menschenmauer | Human Wall, 1960, Bronze, h 37 cm

Familie im Wind I | *Family in the Wind I,* 1967, Bronze, h 46,5 cm

Weibliche Statue II | Female Statue II, 1970/71, Bronze, h 107 cm

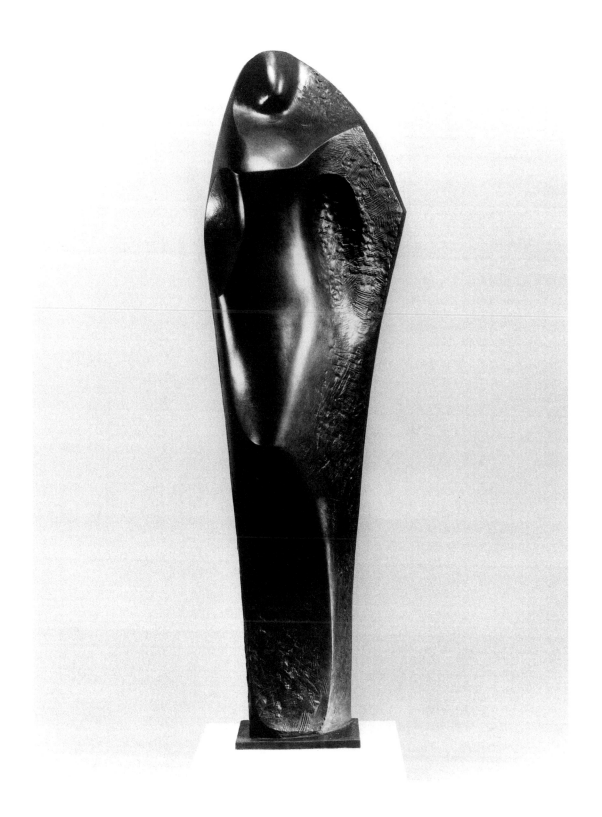

Adams Rippe II | Adam's Rib II, 1967/68, Bronze, h 154 cm

Mauer I | Wall I, 1968, Bronze, h 44 cm

Monument, 1971, Bronze, h 29 cm

Tor | *Gate,* 1970, grüner Marmor und Bronze
green marble and bronze, h 40 cm

Platz I | Place I, 1969, Bronze, h 89 cm

Das Eiland | The Island, 1971, grüner Marmor und vergoldete Bronze
green marble and gilded bronze, h 12 cm

Liegende XVI | Reclining Woman XVI, 1973/74, Bronze, h 38,5 cm

Liegende XVIII | Reclining Woman XVIII, 1974, Bronze, h 20 cm

BERTHOLD

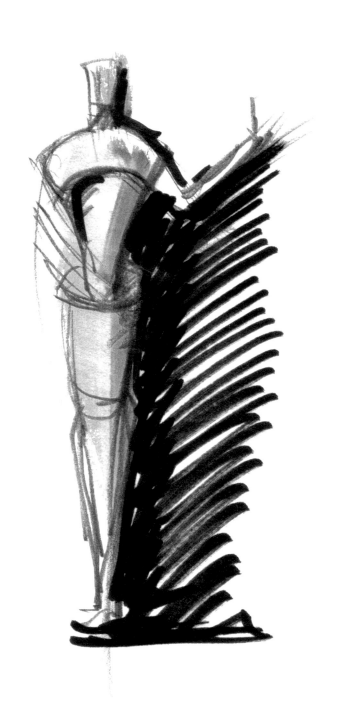

Paar III | Couple III, 1971, Bronze, h 126

Sitzende Frauen | Seated Women, 1972/73, Bronze, h 22 cm

Spiel der Schatten | *Play of the Shadows*, 1973, Bronze, h 47 cm

Mann und Frau in einem Hof sitzend I
Man and Woman seated in a court yard I, 1973, Bronze, h 32 cm

Sitzendes Paar XIV | Seated Couple XIV, 1980, Bronze, h 48 cm

Neuer Adam II | *New Adam II*, 1973, Bronze, h 139 cm

Entwicklung | Development, 1976/77, Bronze, h 40 cm

Schale und Kern | *Shell and Kernel,* 1974, Bronze, h 32 cm

Kegel | Cone, 1976/77, Bronze, h 31 cm

„Die Spannung eines Kunstwerkes ergibt sich durch kompositorischen Gegensatz. In der Skulptur spricht man auch von Gegenbewegung. Die allgemein bekannte Bewegung ist der Wechsel von Stand- und Spielbein bei einer stehenden Figur und die entgegengesetzte Drehung von Becken und Schulter. Desgleichen gibt die erstmals von Donatello in seinem *St. Georg* nur in seinem Becken verwendete gegensätzliche Drehung eines Körpers einer Skulptur Spannung und Kraft. Ebenso sorgen unterschiedliche Behandlung der Oberfläche, der Wechsel oder das Gegeneinanderstellen von rauher und glatter Oberfläche für Bewegung, welche der Betrachter als anregend empfindet. Spannung bedeutet in der Darstellung von Mann und Frau allein schon die Verschiedenheit der Geschlechter. Trotz der betonten Symmetrie in Haltung und Bewegung der Gliedmaßen und der dadurch von ihnen ausgehenden Ruhe ist auch in den ägyptischen Paaren dieses Spannungsmoment vorhanden. Da Mann und Frau gemeinsam dargestellt sind, werden Assoziationen wie Zuneigung und Zusammenhalt hervorgerufen, die Anteilnahme erwecken.“

'The tension in a work of art is created by opposites in its composition. In sculpture one speaks also of contrary movement. The movement which is known to everyone is the alternation between the supporting and the moving leg in a standing figure and the rotation of pelvis and shoulders in opposite directions. A similar effect of strength and tension is produced by the contrary turning of a body using the pelvis alone, first used by Donatello in his *St. George*. Also, the various treatments of the surface, the alternation or juxtaposition of rough and smooth surfaces, produce movement which attracts the interest of the viewer. Tension is created in depictions of man and woman through the difference in gender alone. Despite stressing symmetry in posture and the movement of the limbs, and despite the stillness which arises from this, this moment of tension is present even in the Egyptian sculptures of couples. As man and woman are depicted together, associations such as attraction and solidarity are evoked and this calls up sympathy.'

JOACHIM BERTHOLD, 1988

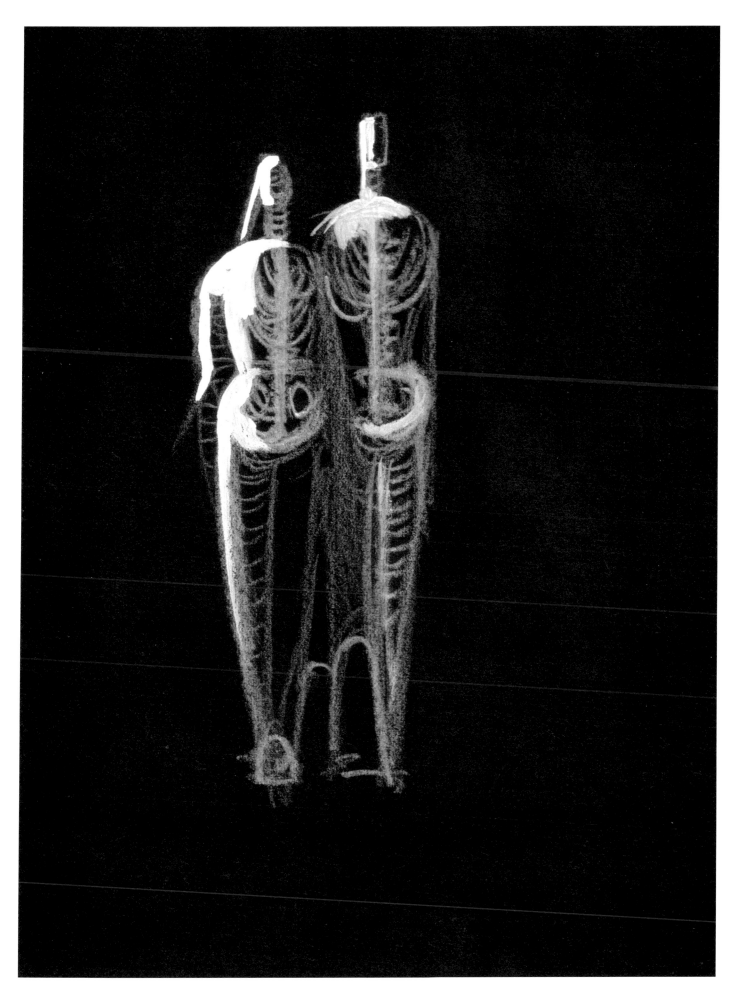

Genese I | Genesis I, 1976/77, Bronze, h 37,5 cm

Die Hälfte einer Kapsel | The Half of a Capsul, 1979, Bronze, h 48 cm

Diskos, 1979, Bronze, h 22 cm

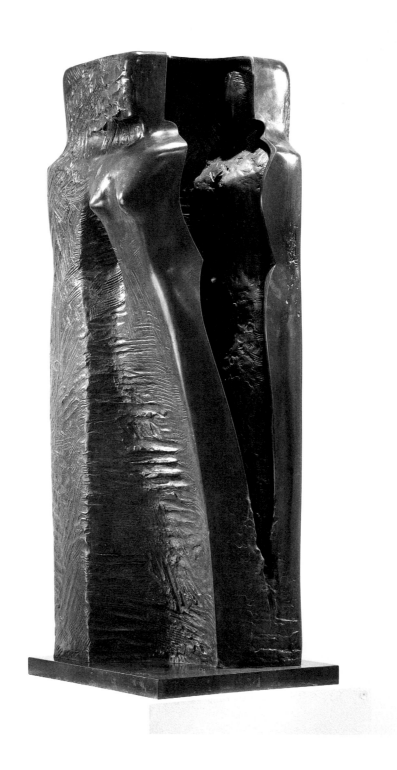

Form aus Form | Form from Form, 1978/79, Bronze, h 115 cm

Des Schattens Arm | The Shadow's Arm, 1979, Bronze, h 62,5 cm

„Der Mensch muß sich in seinem Leben, diesem Zeitraum zwischen Geburt und Tod, behaupten. Er besitzt hierzu eine Vielfalt von körperlichen und geistigen Eigenschaften, deren Gegensätzlichkeit zu großen Spannungen und Katastrophen führen kann. Vor allem jedoch gibt ihm die Fähigkeit, schöpferisch tätig zu sein, die im irdischen Bereich nur er besitzt und die ihn als geistiges Wesen auszeichnet, die Möglichkeit, sich sowohl im physischen Bereich einzurichten als auch die metaphysische Dimensionen zu erahnen, aus denen er kommt oder in die er geht. Er findet im Ergebnis des schöpferischen Tuns die Bestätigung für den Wert seines Lebens. Wenn er das Wesen des Seins nur mit dem Verstand zu erfassen versucht, wird ihm die Spanne zwischen Geburt und Tod leicht als sinnlos erscheinen." ...

„Als Gymnasiast war ich sehr beeindruckt vom Höhlengleichnis in Platons *Staat,* das ich damals selbstverständlich in seiner ganzen Bedeutung nicht erfaßte. Obwohl ich mich in den späteren Jahren nicht mehr damit beschäftigte, muß es in meinem Unterbewußtsein etwas angerührt haben, das meine Auffassung vom Wesen des Daseins prägte, oder es hat in mir eine Anlage für diese Anschauungen vorgefunden. Wenn ich nun meine, daß der Wechsel von Positiv und Negativ innerhalb meiner Plastiken (und zwar innerhalb einer Plastik) die Dimension der wahren Realität darstellt und somit nicht allein ein formales Problem, sondern ein existentielles Moment ist, so ist das eine Feststellung nach der Formfindung. Beispiele für diese Anschauung sind *Rotunda, Läufer, Schreitender, Spiel der Schatten, Drei Schatten.* Auch meine Platz- und Raumgestaltun-

'Man must, during his space of time between birth and death, hold his own. For this purpose he is equipped with a multiplicity of physical and mental qualities whose contrariety can lead to considerable tensions and catastrophes. Primarily, though, it is his capacity to be actively creative, which in the terrestrial sphere he alone possesses and which stamps him as a spiritual being, that enables him to accommodate himself to the world's physical conditions as well as to sense the metaphysical dimensions from which he has come or in which he is proceeding. The yield of his creative activity corroborates for him that life is worthwhile. Should he try solely by intellect to grasp the intrinsic property of being, the span between birth and death will seem somewhat absurd or senseless.' ...

'At high school I was greatly impressed by the simile of the cave in Plato's *Republic.* Naturally at that time I did not discern its full significance. In later years it no longer filled my mind. Nonetheless in my subconscious it must have stirred something that moulded my inter-

Auszug aus der Rede Joachim Bertholds zur Eröffnung seiner Einzelausstellung im Vancouver Centennial Museum, Vancouver, B.C., am 1. Dezember 1977

Excerpt from Joachim Berthold's speech at the opening of his one-man exhibition at the Vancouver Centennial Museum, Vancouver, B.C., on December 1st, 1977

gen mit dem Gegenüber von Mensch und Objekt wie *Platz II, Objekt I,* und die Idee der Menschenmauer, wie sie sich in *Mauer 1968, Mauer IV* darstellt bis zu ihren Abwandlungen in der stelenartigen Form bei den Plastiken *Schreitender* und *Neuer Adam,* sind als geformte Erkenntnis zur menschlichen Existenz anzusehen.

Meine Arbeit geht somit nicht von Inhalten aus, sie wächst und reift bis zur Übereinstimmung von künstlerischer Form und Inhalt. Die Form muß den Künstler bewegen und das Werk ist dann gelungen, wenn seine Aussage an den von ihm gestalteten Formen abzulesen ist und daraus das Allgemeingültige spricht."

pretation of life's substance or must have encountered within me a predisposition towards this interpretation. If in my view the oscillation of positive and negative in the recesses of my sculptures (inside a single specimen, indeed) represents the dimension of true reality, and therefore is not alone a problem of form but an instant of quintessential existence, then this is an inference following discovery of the form. Examples for this kind of vision are *Rotunda, Runner, Pacing Man, Play of the Shadows, Three Shadows.*

My configurations too of place and space, with their contraposition between man and object as in *Place II, Object I,* and the idea of the human wall as in *Wall 1968, Wall IV,* should in all their variations, including the stele-like form in *Pacing Man* and *New Adam,* be regarded as modelled perceptions on the subject of man's existence.'

BERTHOLD

Schreitender III | Pacing Man III, 1979, Bronze, h 43 cm

„Ich spreche ja keinesfalls davon, daß die Verzerrungen oder Deformierungen des menschlichen Körpers nicht Kunst sind oder sein können. Es ist manchmal leicht, einen Ausdruck oder eine gewisse Interessantheit dadurch zu erreichen, daß ich deformiere, das heißt, daß ich die Form zertrümmere. So wie eine geborstene griechische Säule, die allein in den Himmel ragt, uns beeindruckt, so wie ein Torso uns oft mehr berührt als eine fertige Figur.

Vielleicht ist es eine bestimmte Saite, die dadurch in unserem Innern angerührt wird, die Saite, die erklingt, wenn wir spüren, daß unser Leben nicht vollkommen ist, sondern stets nur ein Wollen und Streben nach dem Vollkommenen. Viel schwieriger ist es dagegen, einen Ausdruck zu erreichen, der sofort unser Empfindungsvermögen ansprechen kann, wenn wir eine Figur stilisieren, nicht deformieren, wenn wir die humanen Formen in ihrer Ordnung bestehen und die Figur in ihrer Ganzheit vor uns erstehen lassen.

Wie ich schon sagte, habe ich nicht die Ansicht, daß der Künstler grundsätzlich nicht deformieren oder daß er vom Torso ablassen soll. Jede Art der Form hat ihre Berechtigung. Ihre Berechtigung aus der echten künstlerischen Kraft, die sie gestaltet, und der jeweils neu gestellten Aufgabe, die jede neu begonnene Plastik ist. Ich meine, während die eine Plastik zur Erreichung des Ausdrucks deformierte menschliche Formen benötigt, benötigt die andere die Erhaltung des menschlichen Erscheinungsbildes.

Weder das eine noch das andere ist ‚unzeitgemäß' oder ‚zeitgemäß'. Zeitgemäß ist, solange der Mensch existiert und sich seiner Würde bewußt ist, das Menschenbild. Nicht das Abbild, das wissen wir alle. Das Bild des Menschen, das uns sein Wesen zeigt.

Daß wir den Menschen mit heutigen Formmitteln darstellen müssen, ist klar. Aber jede Form muß ihre innere Begründung haben. Wenn sie lediglich um der Form willen gemacht wird, ist sie nichts weiter als ein Arrangement im Sinne des Arrangements der Musik."

'I certainly do not claim that the ruptures or deformations of the human body are not or could not be art. It is often easy to achieve a particular expression or a certain degree of interest by deforming, that is, by destroying the form. Just like a broken Greek column reaching up alone into the sky impresses us, just like a torso often moves us more than a finished figure.

Perhaps this plucks a particular string in our souls, the string which sounds when we sense that our life is not itself whole, but only ever a desire and pursuit of the whole. It is far more difficult, however, to achieve an expression which can immediately engage with our capacity to respond, if we stylise a figure, rather than deform it, if we allow the human forms to exist in order and the figure to appear before us in its totality.

As I said already, I do not take the view that the artist should not, in principle, deform or must avoid the torso. Every kind of form has its own justification. A justification derived from the sincere artistic force which forms it and from the brand new task, which every newly begun sculpture is. I believe that while one sculpture requires deformed human forms to achieve its expression, others require the retention of the human appearance.

Neither the one nor the other is „anachronistic" or „contemporary". The human form will always be contemporary as long as Man exists and is aware of his worth. Not mere illustration, we all know that. The image of the human being which shows to us his essence.

That we must represent humans with present-day resources in form is clear. But every form must have its inner basis. If it was made merely for the sake of the form, it is no more than an arrangement, in the sense of a musical arrangement.'

JOACHIM BERTHOLD, 15. September 1960

BERTHOLD

Weibliche Statue IV
Female Statue IV, 1981
Bronze, h 61 cm

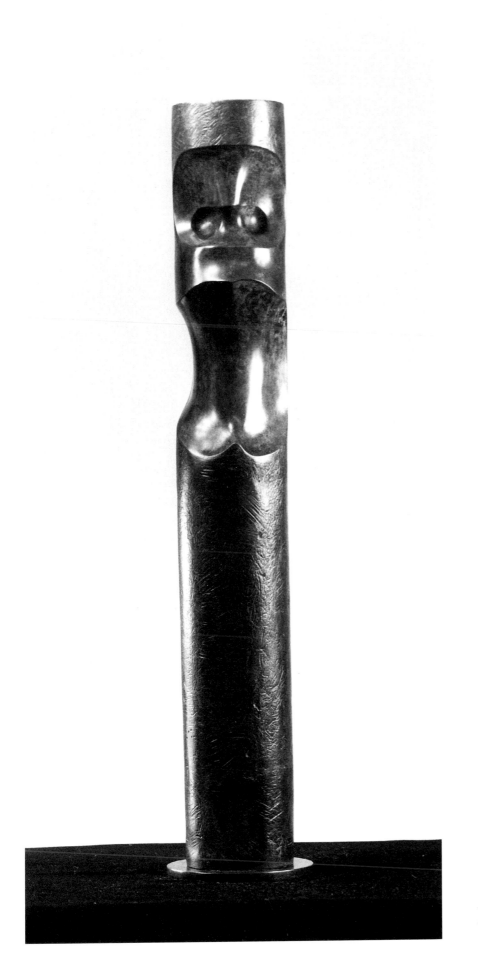

Männliche Statue I
Male Statue I, 1981
Bronze, h 61 cm

Selbdritt | By Three, 1983, Bronze, h 51 cm

Lösung | Separation, 1980, Bronze, h 64 cm

Schatten im Kreis | Shadow in a Circle, 1982, Bronze, h 41 cm

Pieta II, 1989, Bronze, h 32 cm

Platz IV | Place IV, 1983, Bronze, h 20 cm

Verwandlung einer Kugel | Transformation of a Sphere, 1986/89, Bronze, h 77,5 cm

VITA | BIOGRAPHY

AUSSTELLUNGEN | EXHIBITIONS

LITERATUR | LITERATURE

INDEX

VITA

Verfasst von ELFI DAXER, Oberaudorf

BIOGRAPHY

Compiled by ELFI DAXER, Oberaudorf

1917–1936

Joachim Berthold wurde am 17. Oktober 1917, im vorletzten Jahr des Ersten Weltkriegs, in Eisenach geboren. Seine Mutter Maria, Tochter des Bildhauers Georg Kugel, war Malerin und erteilte an der dortigen Großherzoglichen Zeichenschule Zeichenunterricht, um den Lebensunterhalt für sich und ihre drei Kinder zu verdienen. Sein Vater, Karl Berthold, befand sich im Krieg. Er war ein namhafter Goldschmied, der einer Rosenheimer Goldschmiedefamilie entstammte. Nach dem Krieg betätigten sich beide Elternteile, den Wohnsitz öfter wechselnd, weiterhin künstlerisch. Die musische Atmosphäre des Elternhauses und dessen Künstlerfreunde prägten schon die Kindheit Joachim Bertholds, während er die *Deutsche Kunst und Dekoration,* Alexander Kochs Kunstzeitschrift der 1920er und Anfang 1930er Jahre, wie ein Bilderbuch benutzte. De Chirico, Picasso, Barlach, Pechstein und viele andere Künstler waren ihm daher früh ein Begriff. Später gaben ihm die großen Dichtungen der deutschen Literatur aus der elterlichen Bibliothek den Lesestoff. Seine Vorliebe galt Egmont und Torquato Tasso. – Von Jugend an stand für Joachim Berthold fest, Bildhauer zu werden.

Am Friedrich-Wilhelm-Gymnasium Köln machte er 1936 sein Abitur. Damals wurde er mit Plato und dessen *Höhlengleichnis* bekannt, das sich auf sein späteres künstlerisches Schaffen auswirken sollte.[1]

1917–1936

Joachim Berthold was born in Eisenach on October 17, 1917, the year before the First World War ended. His mother Maria, the daughter of the sculptor Georg Kugel was a painter and taught drawing at the Großherzogliche Zeichenschule, Eisenach, to support herself and her three children. Berthold's father Karl was away at the war. He was a renowned goldsmith, a member of a family of goldsmiths from Rosenheim. After the war, both parents pursued artistic careers, with frequent changes of residence. The artistic atmosphere of the parental home and the circle of artists who frequented it were already an influence on Joachim Berthold in his childhood, during which he used Alexander Koch's art magazine of the 1920s and early 1930s, *Deutsche Kunst und Dekoration*, as if it were a child's picture book. De Chirico, Picasso, Barlach, Pechstein and many other artists thus became familiar to him. Later he found his reading material in the great works of German literature in his parents' library. His favourites were Goethe's *Egmont* and *Torquato Tasso*. Right from his early years it was clear that Joachim Berthold would be a sculptor.

He completed his schooling in 1936 with an *Abitur* at the Friedrich Wilhelm Gymnasium in Cologne. At that time he became familiar with Plato and his *Allegory of the Cave*, which would influence Berthold's later artistic work.[1]

Die Bildhauerklasse der Kölner Werkschule Weihnachten 1937/38. Zweiter und Dritte von rechts nach links sind Joachim Berthold und Gisela Sames, seine spätere Frau
    The sculpture class of the Werkschule in Cologne, Christmas 1937/38; second and third from right, Joachim Berthold and Gisela Sames, later his wife

1937 in Paris, der angehende Künstler (Mitte) mit Freunden vor dem Invalidendom
    1937 in Paris, the young artist (centre) with friends in front of Les Invalides

1936–1941

Sein Studium als Bildhauer begann Berthold an der Kölner Werkschule. Er arbeitete dort in Holz und Stein, auch in Terrakotta und Gips und erfuhr eine gute Schulung in der Bearbeitung von Bronze und anderen Metallen. Das Studium der Anatomie befand sich ebenso im Lehrplan wie das Studium nach der Natur. Sein Lehrer an der Kölner Werkschule war Wolfgang Wallner, der für ihn zwar kein Vorbild als Künstler war, den er aber als sehr guten Mentor schätzte. – In der Bildhauerklasse lernte er in der Kollegin Gisela Sames seine spätere Frau kennen.

In dieser Zeit ergab sich eine Gelegenheit, nach Paris zu reisen, in Anbetracht der politischen Verhältnisse in Deutschland ein seltener Glücksfall. Man schrieb das Jahr 1937. Berthold nutzte den Aufenthalt in Paris zum Besuch der Museen und aller Stätten und Ateliers, in denen es Kunst zu sehen gab, und zum Kennenlernen von Persönlichkeiten, für die er eine Empfehlung besaß. In der damaligen Weltausstellung sah er Picassos *Guernica* und die Skulptur eines weiblichen Kopfes, und im rumänischen Pavillon entdeckte er die polierte Bronze *L'Oiselet* von Brancusi. Im Hotel Biron und in Meudon erregten Rodins Werke seine große Bewunderung. Da schon immer figürliche Imaginationen seine Vorstellung von Skulptur waren, machten Rodin und Brancusi einen gewaltigen Eindruck auf ihn. Die *Sklaven* von Michelangelo im Louvre vermittelten ihm die Ausdruckskraft eines Genies, dessen Spuren zu Rodin führten.

Beim Weiterstudium an der Akademie der Bildenden Künste in München hatte er, nach der gründlichen handwerklichen Ausbildung in Köln, nicht das Gefühl, noch viel

1936–1941

Berthold began his studies as a sculptor at the Werkschule in Cologne. There he worked in wood and stone, as well as terracotta and plaster, and he received a thorough training in the working of bronze and other metals. The study of anatomy was also on the curriculum, as were studies from nature. His teacher at the Werkschule in Cologne was Wolfgang Wallner, who was no role model for Berthold as an artist but someone he always valued as an excellent mentor. One of his colleagues in the sculpture class was Gisela Sames, later his wife.

During this period he got the chance to travel to Paris – a rare piece of good fortune, considering the political situation in Germany. The year was 1937. Berthold used his stay in Paris to visit the museums and all the venues and studios where art could be viewed, and he made the acquaintance of people to whom he had been recommended. In the World Exhibition at that time he saw Picasso's *Guernica* and his sculpture of a female head and in the Romanian pavilion he discovered Brancusi's polished bronze *L'Oiselet*. In the Hotel Biron and in Meudon he encountered Rodin's works, which earned his great admiration. Because his idea of sculpture had always been figurative, Rodin and Brancusi made a huge impression on him. Michelangelo's *Slaves* in the Louvre showed him the expressive power of a genius whose influence could be traced to Rodin.

In his further studies at the Akademie der Bildenden Künste in Munich, he felt that, after his thorough practical training in Cologne, he had little to learn. He had

Oberaudorf am Inn, von 1940 bis 1990 war es der Wohnsitz des Künstlers
Oberaudorf am Inn, the sculptor's home from 1940 to 1990

Das 1950 erbaute Atelierhaus. Der Wohnteil ist nach Süden gerichtet mit Blick auf den Wilden Kaiser, das Atelier liegt nach Norden
The artist's home and studio, built in 1950; the residential part faces south towards the 'Wilde Kaiser', a range of Alpine peaks; the studio is on the northern side

lernen zu können. Er war Schüler von Josef Wackerle geworden, der in Porzellan Bleibendes geschaffen hatte, und den er den anderen dort lehrenden und zeitbezogenen Professoren vorzog. Seine eigentlichen Maßstäbe hatten ihm Rodin und Brancusi gesetzt. – Der Lehrbetrieb an der Akademie bestand vor allem aus Akt- und Porträtmodellieren nach der Natur, das ihm leicht von der Hand ging. Da er die Körperstudien in Skulpturen eigener Vorstellungen umsetzen wollte, was verpönt war, wurde er als schwieriger Schüler angesehen. Mit diesem Dilemma hatte er schon in Köln zu tun, da er entsprechend seiner Altersstufe und seiner ausgeprägten schöpferischen Fantasie eigene Formerfindungen zu verwirklichen trachtete, während an den Schulen das Handwerk im Vordergrund stand. Er erkannte bald, dass wohl Handwerk an einer Schule gelehrt werden kann, aber die Straße zur Kunst allein gegangen werden muss.

1940 heirateten Joachim Berthold und Gisela Sames und wählten Oberaudorf im Inntal zum Domizil, nicht weit von München entfernt und nahe der väterlichen Heimat. Im Jahr darauf wurde die Tochter Ursula geboren.

1941–1945

Die Zeit an der Akademie war kurz bemessen, denn die Kriegs-Maschinerie des Zweiten Weltkriegs war in vollem Gang, und auch Berthold wurde als Soldat eingezogen. Gelegenheit zur künstlerischen Arbeit fand er nur in den kurzen Urlauben während des Krieges, in denen kleinere expressive Skulpturen in Wachs entstanden, die mit

become a student of Josef Wackerle, who had produced work of lasting value in porcelain and whom Berthold preferred to the other professors at the academy, who were very much of their time. His own personal standards had been set by Rodin and Brancusi. The teaching at the Academy consisted above all of nude and portrait modelling from life, which he carried out with ease. Because he wished to develop the figure studies into sculptures after his own ideas – something that was unacceptable at that time – he was regarded as a difficult student. He had already had to deal with this dilemma in Cologne, where, as befitted his age and his strikingly creative imagination, he wished to achieve forms derived from his own imagination, whereas the school's main focus was on practical skills. He soon realised that though practical skills may be learned in a school, the road to art must be travelled alone.

In 1940 Joachim Berthold and Gisela Sames married and chose as their home Oberaudorf in the Inn Valley, not far from Munich and near the hometown of Berthold's father. In the following year their daughter Ursula was born.

1941–1945

Berthold's time at the Academy was to be short-lived as the war machine of the Second World War was running at full speed and Berthold too was called up as a soldier. His only opportunity for artistic work came during his short holidays from the war effort, in which he created small, expressive sculptures in wax which did not comply

Sommer 1954, auf der Terrasse des Atelierhauses. Joachim Berthold und Gisela Berthold-Sames mit den Töchtern Ursula und Sabine
Summer 1954, on the terrace of the studio-house: Joachim Berthold and Gisela Berthold-Sames with their daughters Ursula and Sabine

Einzelausstellung Bertholds in der Städtischen Galerie im Lenbachhaus, München. Eröffnung am 1. Dezember 1961
Solo exhibition by Berthold in the Städtische Galerie im Lenbachhaus, Munich; the opening on December 1, 1961

Das *Menschenpaar* von 1958 auf der 7. Biennale voor Beeldhouwkunst im Middelheimpark, Antwerpen 1963
Menschenpaar (Human Couple) from 1958 at the 7th *Biennale voor Beeldhouwkunst* at the Middelheimpark, Antwerp 1963

den damaligen staatlichen Vorgaben für die
Schönheit in der Kunst nicht übereinstimm-
ten, und die weder vorgezeigt noch ausge-
stellt werden konnten. Das war ihm ebenso
gleichgültig, wie er auch in der Nachkriegs-
zeit, als die Darstellung des Menschen als
unzeitgemäß galt, unbeirrt seinen eigenen
künstlerischen Intentionen nachging.

1945–1959
Nach Beendigung des Krieges bot sich dem
jungen Bildhauer Gelegenheit, in einer
Töpferwerkstatt in Oberaudorf ein erstes
Atelier einzurichten. Da in dieser Zeit jede
Brotarbeit ausgeführt werden musste, konnte er sich nur in bescheidenem Maß seiner
künstlerischen Entwicklung widmen. Ge-
hilfen und Schüler gingen ihm bei den Auf-
trägen zur Hand. Als das sehr kleine Atelier
zu eng wurde und sich ihm die Möglichkeit
bot, im Schloss Reisach bei Oberaudorf grö-
ßere Räume zu beziehen, richtete er sich
dort ein. Bald musste er diese wieder auf-
geben, weil das Schloss verkauft wurde. Er
sah sich zum Bau eines eigenen Ateliers ge-
zwungen, das 1950 entstand und gleichzeitig Wohnhaus wurde. Die in diesen Jahren
schwierige wirtschaftliche Lage in Deutschland machte es ihm nicht leicht, sowohl für
die Familie zu sorgen, die sich 1953 durch
die Geburt der Tochter Sabine vergrößert
hatte, als auch sein Vorhaben weiterzuver-
folgen, Kunst von Rang und bleibendem
Wert zu schaffen. Zielstrebig unterschied er
weiterhin zwischen Auftragsarbeiten, die er
gewissenhaft ausführe, und den Werken im
eigenen Auftrag, an denen er sich erproben
konnte.

with the state's prescriptions for beauty in
art and which therefore could not be displayed or exhibited. This did not trouble
him, just as after the war, when the representation of the human form was regarded
as anachronistic, he pursued his own artistic intentions without wavering.

1945–1959
After the war was over, the young sculptor was able to set up his first studio, in a
pottery workshop in Oberaudorf. During
this period he was obliged to take on every
available commission to support himself
and so was only able to pursue his artistic
development to a limited degree. Assistants
and pupils assisted him with the commissions. When the tiny studio was no longer
large enough, the opportunity arose of tak-
ing over bigger premises in Schloss Reisach,
a castle near Oberaudorf, and he set up a
studio there; he soon had to give this up,
however, when the castle was sold. He felt
obliged to build his own studio, which he
completed in 1950, making it also his home.
The economic situation in Germany at this
time was very difficult so it was not an easy
task to provide for his family - now also including his daughter Sabine, born in 1953 -
while also pursuing his ambition of creating
art of quality and lasting worth. Focusing
on his main goal, he distinguished clearly
between commissions, which he dutifully
completed, and works which he carried out
for himself, in which he could test himself.

Schaufenster der David B. Findlay Galleries,
New York, zur ersten Einzelausstellung in
den USA im Oktober 1966
   Window of the David B. Findlay Galleries,
   New York, at the first solo exhibition in the
   USA in October 1966

Eine der weiteren Ausstellungen in den David
B. Findlay Galleries
   Another of the exhibitions at the David B.
   Findlay Galleries

Joachim Berthold in New York

Der Bogen war zunächst weit gespannt: Bizarres mischte sich mit Urformen, Ekstatisches stand neben architektonisch gebauten Elementen. Es entwickelte sich Bertholds zentrales Anliegen: „Die Form ist ihm Träger und Gehäuse eines geläuterten Menschenbildes. Berthold will mit seiner Kunst nicht die Erscheinungsform, sondern das Wesen der Dinge zeigen".[2]

1960–1964

Joachim Berthold stellte in der Folge den Menschen nicht mehr nur als Einzelwesen, sondern als Paar und als Angehörigen einer Gemeinschaft dar, was 1960 in den Kompositionen *Menschenmauer* und *Memento* ihre Entsprechung fand. Diese beiden Skulpturen gehörten dann auch zu den Arbeiten, mit denen er erstmals in die Öffentlichkeit trat. Mehrere Museen (Landesmuseum für Kunst und Kulturgeschichte in Münster, Städtische Galerie im Lenbachhaus in München, Suermondt-Ludwig-Museum in Aachen u. a.) führten Einzelausstellungen durch, die ihn einem größeren Publikum bekannt machten. Es folgten Einladungen zu Ausstellungen im Ausland, so nach Paris zum *Salon de la Jeune Sculpture,* zum *Salon des Grands et Jeunes d'Aujourdhui* und 1963 zur Teilnahme an der 7. *Biennale voor Beeldhowkunst* in Antwerpen.

Herbert Read wurde auf das Werk von Joachim Berthold aufmerksam und würdigte sein Schaffen durch Veröffentlichung der Bronzeskulptur *Gebeugter* von 1960 in seiner 1964 erschienenen *A Concise History of Modern Sculpture.*[3] Im gleichen Jahr kam in Deutschland der Band *Plastik der Gegenwart* heraus, in dem Ulrich Gertz die *Menschenmauer* vorstellte.

At first he cast a wide net: the bizarre was combined with primeval forms, the ecstatic appeared alongside architectonic elements. Out of this, Berthold's central artistic focus developed: 'For him, form supports and houses a pristine image of Man. Berthold wants to show not the appearance but the essence of things in his art.'[2]

1960–1964

Thereafter, Joachim Berthold no longer presented the human figure as a single individual, but as a couple or as a member of a group. This development was expressed in his 1960 compositions *Human Wall* and *Memento*. These two sculptures were among those which he first exhibited in public. A number of museums (including the Landesmuseum für Kunst und Kulturgeschichte in Münster, the Städtische Galerie im Lenbachhaus in Munich and the Suermondt Ludwig Museum in Aachen) presented solo exhibitions, which brought him to the attention of the public. Thereafter he was invited to participate in exhibitions abroad, such as the *Salon de la Jeune Sculpture* and the *Salon des Grands et Jeunes d'Aujourd'hui* in Paris, and in 1963 he was invited to take part in the 7th *Biennale voor Beeldhowkunst* in Antwerp.

Herbert Read became aware of Joachim Berthold's work and paid tribute to it by publishing the 1960 bronze sculpture *Bowed Man* in his book *A Concise History of Modern Sculpture* (1964).[3] In the same year, Ulrich Gertz's *Plastik der Gegenwart*, depicting *Human Wall*, was also published.

Blick in eine Einzelausstellung Bertholds in der Gimpel/Weitzenhoffer Gallery, New York
View of a solo exhibition by Berthold at the Gimpel Weitzenhoffer Gallery, New York

Bertholds Bronze *Drei Schatten* in Manhattan, im Vordergrund die Silhouette des Künstlers
Berthold's bronze *Three Shadows* in Manhattan; in the foreground is the sculptor's silhouette

Seit 1965

Ende 1965 trat der New Yorker Kunsthändler A. Max Weitzenhoffer mit Berthold in
Verbindung, suchte ihn kurz darauf selbst
auf und kaufte en bloc alle im Atelier
vorhandenen Skulpturen für die David B.
Findlay Galleries, um die ersten Einzelausstellungen des Künstlers in New York zu
veranstalten. Als sich Weitzenhoffer mit der
Gimpel Weitzenhoffer Gallery selbstständig machte, übernahm diese ebenfalls die
Werke Bertholds. Mittlerweile hatte auch
der Sammler und Kunsthändler Francis C.
Reif in Vancouver, B.C., begonnen, Arbeiten Bertholds zu erwerben, um sich für sie
in Kanada einzusetzen.

Der Aufenthalt in New York anlässlich
der ersten Einzelausstellung im Jahre 1966
vermittelte dem Künstler entscheidende
Eindrücke, welche die maßgebliche Phase
seines Schaffens einleiteten. Er schreibt in
einem Essay „Die Idee der Menschenmauern": „Im Jahre 1966 kam ich anlässlich
meiner ersten Ausstellung nach New York
und damit auch das erste Mal nach Ame-
rika. Weitere Aufenthalte schlossen sich
an. Nach einiger Zeit sah ich an meiner Arbeit, daß sie einen entscheidenden Impuls
erhalten hatte und daß mir die Jahre 1967
und 1968 – es sind die Entstehungsjahre der
Mauer I von 1968 – die völlige künstlerische
Unabhängigkeit gebracht hatten. Ich hatte
Neues erlebt und erfand Neues, ohne daß
eine der Kunstrichtungen der sechziger
Jahre daran Anteil gehabt hätte. Die ame-
rikanische Umwelt vermittelte mir Arche-
typisches in anderer Weise. Die Dynamik
New Yorks faszinierte mich, und sie faszi-

After 1965

At the end of 1965, the New York art dealer
A. Max Weitzenhoffer made contact with
Berthold, visited him in person soon after,
and bought up *en bloc* all the sculptures in
his studio for the David B. Findlay Galleries
to put on Berthold's first solo show in New
York. When Weitzenhoffer set up on his own
with the Gimpel Weitzenhoffer Gallery, this
gallery took over Berthold's works. In the
meantime, the collector and dealer Francis
C. Reif in Vancouver, B.C. had begun to ac-
quire works by Berthold to promote him in
Canada.

Berthold's visit to New York for the first
solo show in 1966 made a lasting impression on him and ushered in the definitive
phase of his career. In an essay entitled
"The Idea of Human Walls", he wrote: 'In
1966 I came to New York for my first exhibition, which was also my first time in America. More visits followed. After a while, I
noticed in my work that it had received a
decisive stimulus and that for me the years
1967 and 1968 – that is, the years in which
the *Wall I* of 1968 was created – had brought
me complete artistic independence. I had
experienced new things and I discovered
new things, though none of the artistic
trends of the sixties played any part in that.
The world of America conveyed archetypes
to me in a novel way. The dynamism of New
York fascinated me and it has continued to
fascinate me ever since. Many of my previ-

Einzelausstellung Galerie Gmurzynska,
Köln
    Solo exhibition Galerie Gmurzynska,
    Cologne

Gisela Berthold-Sames

92

niert mich immer wieder. Viele bisherige Wertungen und Größenordnungen und die bisherige Geborgenheit in der oberbayerischen Landschaft, in der ich lebe, werden durch diese Erfahrungen relativiert. Ich löste mich vom Bisherigen und tauchte ein in ein Gefühl der Zeitlosigkeit angesichts krassen Absterbens und vitalen Werdens, und erhielt dadurch die erweiterte Schau des Seins auf welcher die Entdeckung neuer Formen beruht." – Die *Mauer I* von 1968 gilt als Bertholds Schlüsselwerk.

1967

Als erste im deutschen Kunsthandel arrangierte Antonina Gmurzynska 1967 eine umfangreiche Einzelausstellung Bertholds in ihrer Kölner Galerie. Darüber hinaus fanden in diesem Jahr weitere Einzelausstellungen und Beteiligungen an Gruppenausstellungen in den Vereinigten Staaten und Kanada (*Expo '67* Montreal) statt.

1970–1975

Der Künstler hatte früh begonnen, seiner Frau Gisela von jeder Skulptur einen Guss zu schenken. So entstand die Sammlung Berthold-Sames, deren wachsender Bestand eigene Räume verlangte. Er errichtete daher im Jahre 1970 neben dem Atelierhaus ein Galeriegebäude, das auch in seinen Gartenanlagen Gelegenheit zur Ausstellung größerer Bronzeskulpturen im Freien bot. Auch war es nun möglich, neue Werke im Wechsel mit älteren Arbeiten zu zeigen und das ständig umfangreicher werdende Archiv mit der Fotothek, den Gipsmodellen und Zeichnungen unterzubringen.

ous values and senses of scale, and my previous immersion in the landscape of Upper Bavaria where I live, became relativised through those experiences. I freed myself from what had gone before and immersed myself in a sense of timelessness in the face of mere dying and vital growing, and through this I acquired a broader view of being, on which the discovery of new forms was based.' Berthold's 1968 *Wall I* is considered his key work.

1967

Antonina Gmurzynska was the first art dealer in Germany to arrange, in 1967, an extensive solo exhibition of Berthold's work, in her gallery in Cologne. Other solo shows and group exhibitions also took place in the United States and Canada (*Expo '67* in Montreal) during the same year.

1970–1975

From early on in his career, the sculptor had presented his wife Gisela with a cast of every one of his sculptures. In this way the Berthold-Sames Collection was created and its growing contents required their own premises. Berthold therefore built a gallery beside the studio-house, which also created the possibility of exhibiting larger bronzes in the open air. It now became possible to show new works alongside older pieces and to house the ever-growing archive, which included photographs, plaster casts and drawings.

Das 1970 neben dem Atelier erbaute Galeriehaus, in dem die in der Sammlung Berthold-Sames vereinigten Werke des Künstlers gezeigt wurden

The gallery building, built in 1970 beside the studio-house, in which were displayed the sculptor's works from the Berthold-Sames Collection

Blick in den Galeriegarten
View of the gallery garden

1976–1986

Die Western Association of Art Museums veranstaltete für Joachim Berthold in den Jahren 1976 bis 1978 eine Wanderausstellung in acht Museen und Galerien der Vereinigten Staaten und Kanadas.

An diese Ausstellungsreihe schlossen sich in den folgenden Jahren weitere Einzel- und Gruppenausstellungen in New York an. Mittlerweile befinden sich einige hundert Werke seiner Hand in amerikanischem Besitz.

Die Geschlossenheit von Bertholds Œuvre und seine weitere Verbreitung liegen im Verfolgen eines geradlinigen künstlerischen Wegs, den auch Ausstellungen der letzten Jahre in Köln, Basel, Frankfurt, sowie weitere Veröffentlichungen und die vermehrten Ankäufe öffentlicher Institutionen und privater Sammler anschaulich machen.

1987

erschien bei Hirmer, München, eine Monografie über den Künstler, zu deren Verfassern Wilhelm F. Arntz, Viola Herms Draht, Ulrich Gertz und Katharina Schneider zählten. Die Herausgabe fiel mit der großen Einzelausstellung in der Städtischen Galerie Rosenheim zusammen, welche die Stadt Rosenheim dem Bildhauer zu seinem siebzigsten Geburtstag gewidmet hatte.

1990–1991

fand eine letzte Einzelausstellung zu Lebzeiten des Künstlers in der Galerie am Lützowplatz in Berlin statt. Joachim Berthold erkrankte kurz nach Beendigung der Ausstellung in Berlin schwer und starb am 25. September 1990 in Rosenheim. Kurz vor seinem Tod erwarb ein japanischer Kunsthändler 25 Bronzeskulpturen und einige Pinselzeichnungen, um diese Auswahl

1976–1986

From 1976 to 1978 the Western Association of Art Museums staged a circulating exhibition of Berthold's work in eight museums and galleries in the United States and Canada. This series of exhibitions was followed by further solo and group shows in New York. By this time, several hundred works by Berthold were in American collections.

The coherence of Berthold's work and its prevalence can be traced to his steady pursuit of one artistic path, as can also be seen in the exhibitions of his final years in Cologne, Basel and Frankfurt and in new publications on the sculptor and an increasing number of acquisitions by public institutions and private collectors.

1987

In this year a monograph on Berthold was issued by the publishers Hirmer in Munich. Its authors included Wilhelm F. Arntz, Viola Herms Draht, Ulrich Gertz and Katharina Schneider. The publication coincided with a major solo exhibition in the Städtische Galerie Rosenheim presented by the town of Rosenheim on the occasion of the sculptor's seventieth birthday.

Das Stanford University Museum of Art, Palo Alto, Kalifornien, veranstaltete im Sommer des Jahres 1978 ebenfalls eine Einzelausstellung Joachim Bertholds
> Stanford University Museum of Art, Palo Alto, California, also staged a solo exhibition by Joachim Berthold in the summer of 1978

Im Dezember 1977 Einzelausstellung im Vancouver Museum, Vancouver, B. C., Canada, die Joachim Berthold mit einer Rede eröffnete, die als *The Vancouver Speech* publiziert wurde
> December 1977, solo exhibition in the Vancouver Museum, Vancouver, B. C., Canada, opened by Joachim Berthold with a speech published as *The Vancouver Speech*

aus dem Werk Joachim Bertholds in einer Ausstellung im Frühjahr 1991 in der Gallery Art Point, Tokio, mit großem Erfolg zu zeigen.

1996–1998

Im Jahre 1996 verstarb Bertholds Ehefrau Gisela Berthold-Sames in Oberaudorf. Zwei Jahre später zeigte seine Tochter Sabine Berthold-Fordemann dort eine kleine Auswahl des Schaffens ihres Vaters im Museum am Burgtor.

2007

Ausgewählte Werke von Joachim Berthold sind anlässlich der 90. Wiederkehr seines Geburtstages in der Samuelis Baumgarte Galerie in Bielefeld zu sehen.

Weitere Ausstellungen sind in Vorbereitung.

1990–1991

A final solo show within the sculptor's lifetime took place in the Galerie am Lützowplatz in Berlin. Joachim Berthold became seriously ill in Berlin shortly after the exhibition ended and died at Rosenheim on September 25, 1990. Shortly before his death a Japanese art dealer acquired 25 bronzes and some brush drawings and displayed this selection of Berthold's work in a highly successful exhibition in the spring of 1991 at the Gallery Art Point, Tokyo.

1996–1998

In 1996 Berthold's wife Gisela Berthold-Sames died in Oberaudorf. Two years later his daughter Sabine Berthold-Fordemann presented a small selection of her father's work at the Museum am Burgtor in Oberaudorf.

2007

A selection of works by Joachim Berthold will be on display at the Samuelis Baumgarte Galerie in Bielefeld, on the occasion of the 90th anniversary of his birth.

Further exhibitions are planned.

Francis C. Reif, der Kunsthändler und Sammler von Bertholds Arbeiten, in seinem Office in Vancouver
Francis C. Reif, art dealer and collector of Berthold's works, in his office in Vancouver

Einzelausstellung zum siebzigsten Geburtstag Joachim Bertholds in der Städtischen Galerie Rosenheim im Oktober 1987. Blick in den Hauptsaal
Solo exhibition for Joachim Berthold's seventieth birthday in the Städtische Galerie Rosenheim in October 1987; view of the main exhibition room

1   JOACHIM BERTHOLD, „Die Idee der Menschenmauern", in: WILHELM F. ARNTZ, JOACHIM BERTHOLD, VIOLA HERMS DRAHT, ULRICH GERTZ, KATHARINA SCHNEIDER, *Joachim Berthold,* München 1987, S. 22
2   ULRICH GERTZ, *Plastik der Gegenwart,* Rembrandt Verlag, Berlin 1964, S. 94, S. 131–132, S. 245
3   HERBERT READ, *A Concise History of Modern Sculpture,* Thames and Hudson, London 1964, S. 181, 288

1   JOACHIM BERTHOLD, "The Idea of Human Walls", in *Leonardo,* Pergamon Press, Oxford/San Francisco, 1984, Vol. 17, pp. 146–151
2   ULRICH GERTZ, *Plastik der Gegenwart,* Rembrandt Verlag, Berlin 1964, pp. 94, 131–132, 245
3   HERBERT READ, *A Concise History of Modern Sculpture,* Thames and Hudson, London 1964, pp. 181, 288

Einzelausstellungen | Solo exhibitions
(Auswahl | Selection)

1960	Leopold-Hoesch-Museum, Düren Landesmuseum für Kunst und Kulturgeschichte, Münster Deutsches Klingenmuseum, Solingen
1961	Städtisches Gustav-Lübcke-Museum, Hamm Städtische Kunstsammlungen, Ludwigshafen Städtische Galerie im Lenbachhaus, München	Munich
1962	Suermondt-Ludwig-Museum, Aachen Städtische Galerie, Rosenheim
1963	Galerie am Dom im Karmeliter-kloster, Frankfurt am Main Museum der Stadt Regensburg
1964	Kunstverein Konstanz
1966	David B. Findlay Galleries, New York
1967	Closson's Gallery, Cincinnati Galerie Gmurzynska, Köln	Cologne
1968	Galleria de Il Giorno, Mailand	Milan Vanderbilt University Fine Arts Gallery, Nashville David B. Findlay Galleries, New York
1970	David B. Findlay Galleries, New York
1971	Museum der Stadt Regensburg
1974	Städtisches Gustav-Lübcke-Museum, Hamm David B. Findlay Galleries, New York Carnegie Center, Walla Walla
1975	Städtische Galerie Würzburg
1976	Masur Museum of Art, Monroe

1977	Dalzell Hatfield Galleries, Los Angeles California Polytechnic State University, Art Gallery, San Luis Obispo Scottsdale Center for the Arts, Scottsdale Vancouver Museum, Vancouver
1978	North Dakota State University Art Gallery, Fargo Stanford University Museum of Art, Palo Alto Leigh Yawkey Woodson Art Museum, Wausau Galerie Bargera, Köln	Cologne
1980	Gimpel/Weitzenhoffer Gallery, New York
1981	Galerie Stolz, Köln	Cologne David B. Findlay Galleries, New York
1982	*Art13'82* Galerie Stolz, Basel Galerie Stolz, Köln	Cologne
1986	Galerie Timm Gierig, Leinwandhaus, Frankfurt am Main
1987	Städtische Galerie Rosenheim
1990	Haus am Lützowplatz, Berlin
1991	Gallery Art Point, Tokio	Tokyo
1998	Museum im Burgtor, Oberaudorf
2007	Samuelis Baumgarte Galerie, Bielefeld

Gruppenausstellungen | Group exhibition
(Auswahl | Selection)

1963	*7. Biennale voor Beeldhouwkunst,* Antwerpen	Antwerp
1964	*XVIe Salon de la Jeune Sculpture,* Paris
1965	Staatliche Graphische Sammlung, München	Munich
1967	Akron Art Institute, Akron Albright-Knox Art Gallery, Buffalo Morgan Knott Gallery, Dallas *Expo '67,* Deutscher Pavillon, Montreal Staatliche Graphische Sammlung, München	Munich
1968	*Pagani, Legnano,* Museo d'Arte Moderna Fondazione, Mailand	Milan *XXe Salon de la Jeune Sculpture,* Paris
1969	Städtische Kunstsammlungen, Ludwigshafen *Xe Salon des Grands et Jeunes d'Aujourd'hui,* Paris
1972	*XIIIe Salon des Grands et Jeunes d'Aujourd'hui,* Paris
1974	*Liebe und Tod,* Neue Galerie der Stadt Aachen und die waage, Burg Stolberg
1975	*Der ausgesparte Mensch,* Städtische Kunsthalle Mannheim
1977	*Art and Contemporary Architecture,* David B. Findlay Galleries, New York
1978	*Joachim Berthold / Ninoru Niizuma,* Gimpel/Weitzenhoffer Gallery, New York
1985	*Sculptors,* Gimpel/Weitzenhoffer Gallery, New York
1986	*Paintings and Sculpture by Gallery Artists,* Gimpel / Weitzenhoffer Gallery, New York

Arbeiten in öffentlichen und privaten
Sammlungen | Works in Public and Privat
Collections (Auswahl | Selection)

Alexander von Humboldt-Stiftung, Bonn
Bayerische Akademie der Wissenschaften,
    Institut für Tieftemperaturforschung,
    München-Garching | Munich
Bayerische Volksbank, München | Munich
Deutsche Botschaft, Monrovia
Deutsche Gesellschaft für Personalführung,
    Düsseldorf
Deutsches Klingenmuseum, Solingen
General Mills Art Collection, Minneapolis
Kreiskrankenhaus Pasing, München |
    Munich
Landesmuseum für Kunst und Kultur-
    geschichte, Münster
Leopold-Hoesch-Museum, Düren
Ludwig-Maximilians-Universität, Chemisch-
    Pharmazeutische Institute und Klinikum
    Großhadern, München | Munich
Masur Museum of Art, Monroe
Münchner Rückversicherungs-Gesellschaft,
    München | Munich

Museum der Stadt Regensburg
Rheinische Braunkohlenwerke AG,
    Köln | Cologne
Sammlung Ludwig, Aachen
Schulzentrum Merseburger Straße,
    München | Munich
Siemens AG, Bocholt
Siemens AG, Erlangen
Siemens AG, München | Munich
Siemens Canada, Montreal
Simmons Art Collection, Atlanta
Staatliche Graphische Sammlung,
    München | Munich
Städtische Galerie Rosenheim
Städtisches Gustav-Lübcke-Museum, Hamm
Städtisches Museum Würzburg
Stanford University Museum of Art,
    Stanford
Technische Universität, Institut für Land-
    verkehrswege, München | Munich
Vanderbilt University Fine Arts Gallery,
    Nashville
Wilhelm-Haak-Museum, Ludwigshafen
Wilhelm-Lehmbruck-Museum, Duisburg

(Auszug | Selection)

HEINZ LEITERMANN, *Joachim Berthold,* Gurlitt Verlag, München/Linz/Berlin | Munich/Linz/Berlin 1957

GIOVANNI CARADENTE, ALFRED P. ZELLER, *knaurs lexikon der modernen plastik,* Droemersche Verlagsanstalt, München | Munich 1961, S. | p. 32

JACOB REISNER, in: JOACHIM BERTHOLD, *Über das Menschenbild in der Plastik der Gegenwart. Briefe des Bildhauers Joachim Berthold an eine Kunstfreundin,* Carl Lange Verlag, Duisburg 1961

CARL BÄNFER, „Vor der Menschenmauer. Zu neuen Plastiken von Joachim Berthold", in: *Die Kunst und das schöne Heim,* München | Munich, November 1962

ULRICH GERTZ, *Rede zu einer Ausstellung von Joachim Berthold,* Städtische Galerie im Lenbachhaus, München | Munich, Carl Lange Verlag, Duisburg 1962

ERNST GÜNTER GRIMME, „Der Bildhauer Joachim Berthold", in: *Die Weltkunst,* S. | p. 17, München | Munich, April 1963

EUGEN DIEM, „Der Bildhauer Joachim Berthold", in: *Speculum Artis,* Heft | number 2, S. | pp. 15–19, Konstanz/Zürich | Constance/Zurich, März/April | March/April 1964

HERBERT READ, *A Concise History of Modern Sculpture,* Thames and Hudson, S. | pp. 181, 288, London 1964

ULRICH GERTZ, *Plastik der Gegenwart,* Rembrandt Verlag, S. | pp. 94, 131–132, 245, Berlin 1964

JANE H. KAY, "Art's New Year, Fishball by Joachim Berthold", in: *The Christian Science Monitor,* Abb. S. | ill. p. 6, Boston, Oktober | October 12, 1966

D'ARS, Joachim Berthold, Nr. | No. 5, S. | pp. 49, 50, 51, Mailand | Milan 1964/65; Vol. IX, Nr. | No. 40, S. | pp. 114–115, Mailand | Milan 1968

JOACHIM BERTHOLD, *Sculptor's Drawings,* Vanderbilt Fine Arts Gallery Vanderbilt University, Nashville 1968

FRITZ NEUGASS, „Joachim Berthold, Liebe zur reinen Form", in: *Die Kunst und das schöne Heim,* S. | pp. 418–419; München | Munich, September 1969

SHELDON WILLIAMS, "Decade of success for Berthold, the Modern Traditionalist", in: *Art and Antiques Weekly,* S. | p. 16; London, 4. Juli | July 4, 1970

GERRIT HENRY, "Joachim Berthold", in: *Art News,* New York, November 1970

JOACHIM BERTHOLD, "My Conception of the Human Wall", in: *Leonardo,* Vol. 3, S. | pp. 269–274, Pergamon Press, Oxford 1970

ULRICH GERTZ, *Joachim Berthold, Steinmetz und Bildhauer,* S. | pp. 677–680, München | Munich, Dezember | December 1972

GRITTA HESSE, *Kunst der jungen Generation,* Amerika-Gedenkbibliothek, Berliner Zentralbibliothek, Berlin 1968, 1970, 1972, 1974

WILHELM F. ARNTZ, WOLFGANG BRAUNFELS, *Joachim Berthold, Katalog der Skulpturen | Catalogue of Sculptures 1947–1973,* Hans Christians Verlag, Hamburg 1974

HEINZ FUCHS, *Der ausgesparte Mensch,* Städtische Kunsthalle Mannheim, S. | pp. 46, 70, Mannheim 1975

WOLFGANG BRAUNFELS, GIGI DOBBS, *Joachim Berthold, Catalogue Circulating One-Man Exhibition,* Western Association of Art Museums, Oakland, Ca., 1976–1978

ANN FADER, *Art and Contemporary Architecture,* Findlay, S. | pp. 2, 5, New York 1977

FRITZ NEUGASS, „Amerikanische Wanderausstellung von Joachim Bertholds bildhauerischem Schaffen", in: *Weltkunst,* S. | p. 1382, München | Munich, Juni | June 1978

VIOLA HERMS DRAHT, "Are Americans interested in ...", in: *Art News,* S. | pp. 84, 87, New York, N.Y., Oktober | October 1978

JOACHIM BERTHOLD, „Die Rede in Vancouver" | "The Vancouver Speech", Vorwort | Foreword Clifford W. Tosdevin, Vancouver, B. C. 1978

JOACHIM BERTHOLD, *My Artist Background,* Ausst.-Kat. Einzelausstellung | Cat. Solo Exhibition, Gimpel/Weitzenhoffer Gallery, New York 1980

VIVIEN RAYNOR, "Joachim Berthold", in: *The New York Times,* S. | p. 27, New York 10. Oktober | October 10, 1980

CHRISTA VON HASSEL, „Joachim Berthold zeigt Plastiken der 70er Jahre in New York", in: *Weltkunst,* S. | pp. 3460, 3462, München | Munich, November 1980

SIEGFRIED SALZMANN, *Das Wilhelm-Lehmbruck-Museum Duisburg, Plastik und Objektkunst,* Bd. II | Vol. II, S. | pp. 209, 342, Verlag Aurel Bongers, Recklinghausen 1981

JOACHIM BERTHOLD, "The Idea of Human Walls", in: *Leonardo, Pergamon Press,* Nr. | Vol. 17, S. | pp. 146–151, Oxford/San Francisco 1984

VIOLA HERMS DRAHT, „Die Sammlung Berthold-Sames. Das Œuvre des Bildhauers Joachim Berthold", in: *Die Kunst,* Nr. | No. 2, S. | pp. 124–129, München | Munich, Februar | February 1985

WILHELM F. ARNTZ, JOACHIM BERTHOLD, VIOLA HERMS DRAHT, ULRICH GERTZ, KATHARINA SCHNEIDER, *Joachim Berthold,* Hirmer Verlag, München | Munich 1987

JOACHIM BERTHOLD, *Menschenpaare, Gedanken zu Skulpturen in einer Sammlung,* Mercator Verlag, Duisburg 1988

PHILIPPE CLÉRIN, *La Sculpture,* Umschlagabbildung | Cover image, S. | pp. 21, 251, Dessain & Tolra, Paris 1988

PHILIPPE CLÉRIN, *Das grosse Buch des Modellierens und Bildhauens,* Umschlagabbildung | Cover image, S. | pp. 27, 257, Verlag Paul Haupt, Bern und | and Stuttgart 1990

GERHARD KOLBERG, *Joachim Berthold,* Ausst.-Kat. | Exhibition catalogue, Haus am Lützowplatz, Berlin 1990

Zitate des Künstlers |
Quotations from the Artist

Umschlagrückseite | Back cover
Joachim Berthold an Joakim Parker, den Sohn seiner kalifornischen Freunde Dale und Tulla Parker, zur Entstehung der Skulptur *Verwandlung einer Kugel* | Letter from Joachim Berthold to Joakim Parker, son of his Californian Friends Dale and Tulla Parker, on the creation of the sculpture *Transforming of a Sphere* 1990, Sammlung Berthold-Sames, Oberaudorf

Seite | page 25, 72
Zitiert aus | cited in: JOACHIM BERTHOLD, *Über das Menschenbild in der Plastik der Gegenwart; Briefe des Bildhauers Joachim Berthold an eine Kunstfreundin;* Carl Lange Verlag, Duisburg 1961

Seite | page 58
Zitiert aus | cited in: JOACHIM BERTHOLD, *Menschenpaare, Gedanken zu Skulpturen in einer Sammlung,* Mercator Verlag, Duisburg, 1988, S. 21

Seite | page 66/67
Auszug aus der Rede Joachim Bertholds zur Eröffnung seiner Einzelausstellung im Vancouver Centennial Museum, Vancouver, B.C., am 1. Dezember 1977 | Excerpt from Joachim Berthold's speech at the opening of his one-man exhibition at the Vancouver Centennial Museum, Vancouver, B.C., on December 1st, 1977

INDEX

Adams Rippe II | Adam's Rib II, 33

Biest | Beast, 21

Das Eiland | The Island, 40/41

Des Schattens Arm | The Shadow's Arm, 65

Die Hälfte einer Kapsel | The Half of a
   Capsul, 61

Diskos, 7, 63

Entwicklung | Development, 54

Familie im Wind I | Family in the Wind I, 31

Flügelwesen | Winged Creatures, 23

Form aus Form | Form from Form, 64

Genese I | Genesis I, 60

Jüngling | Youngling, 20

Karyatide I | Caryatide I, 27

Kegel | Cone, 57

Liegende XVI | Reclining Woman XVI, 42

Liegende XVIII | Reclining Woman XVIII, 43

Lösung | Separation, 77

Mann und Frau in einem Hof sitzend I | Man
   and Woman seated in a court yard I, 50

Männliche Statue I | Male Statue I, 75

Mauer I | Wall I, 34

Mauer V | Wall V, 8

Memento, 9

Menschenmauer | Human Wall, 28/29

Monument, 36

Neuer Adam II | New Adam II, 53

Paar III | Couple III, 45

Paar VII, | Couple VII, 13

Pieta II, 80

Platz I | Place I, 10, 39

Platz IV | Place IV, 81

Schale und Kern | Shell and Kernel, 55

Schatten | Shadow, 26

Schatten im Kreis |Shadow in a Circle, 79

Schreitender III | Pacing Mann III, 11, 69

Selbdritt | By Three, 76

Sitzende Frauen | Seated Women, 47

Sitzendes Paar XIV | Seated Couple XIV, 51

Spiel der Schatten | Play of the Shadows,
   Umschlag, 49

Tor | Gate, 37

Verwandlung einer Kugel | Transformation
   of a Sphere, 6, 83

Vier Wände | Four Walls, 70

Weibliche Statue II | Female Statue II, 32

Weibliche Statue III | Female Statue III, 12

Weibliche Statue IV | Female Statue IV, 74

Zylinder | Cylinder, 14

Dieses Buch erscheint zur Ausstellung *Joachim Berthold* in der Samuelis Baumgarte Galerie zu Ehren der 90. Wiederkehr des Geburtstags des Künstlers, 7. Oktober bis 10. November 2007.

This catalogue is published in conjunction with the exhibition *Joachim Berthold* in the Samuelis Baumgarte Galerie in honour of the 90th anniversary of the sculptor's birth, October 7th to November 10th, 2007.

Samuelis Baumgarte Galerie
Niederwall 10
33602 Bielefeld, Germany
Telefon: +49 (0) 5 21 / 17 35 32
Fax: +49 (0) 5 21 / 5 60 31 25
info@samuelis-baumgarte.com
www.samuelis-baumgarte.com

Herausgeber | Editor: Sabine Berthold-Fordemann, Karl Fordemann, Herford
Lektorat und Koordination | Copyediting and coordination: Tanja Kemmer, Kerber Verlag, Bielefeld
Übersetzungen | Translations: Orla Mulholland, Berlin
Fotonachweis | Photo credits: Roland Bielesch, Bielefeld, (Umschlagabbildung | Cover illustration), Ernst Reinhold, München | Munich (S. | pp. 6, 7, 8, 32, 52, 53, 55, 57, 61, 63, 69, 83), Stephan Baron von Koskull, Rosenheim (S. | p. 2), alle übrigen | all others Sabine Berthold-Fordemann
Gestaltung | Design: Andreas Koch, Bielefeld
Umschlagabbildung | Cover illustration: Spiel der Schatten | Play of the Shadows, 1973, Bronze, h 47 cm

Printed and published by
Kerber Verlag, Bielefeld/Leipzig
Windelsbleicher Straße 166–170
33659 Bielefeld, Germany
Telefon +49 (0) 5 21 / 9 50 08-10
Fax +49 (0) 5 21 / 9 50 08 88
info@kerberverlag.com
www.kerberverlag.com
US Distribution
D.A.P., Distributed Art
Publishers Inc.
155 Sixth Avenue/2nd Floor
New York 10013.1507, USA
Phone 001 212 627 1999
Fax 001 212 627 9484

ISBN 978-3-86678-097-2

Printed in Germany